THESE WORDS UPON
YOUR HEART

THESE WORDS UPON
YOUR HEART

DAILY REFLECTIONS ON
SPIRITUAL CLASSICS

Edited by Paul Ofstedal

Augsburg
MINNEAPOLIS

To Anne, Daniel, Joseph, Ruth,
and my dear wife, Dorothea

THESE WORDS UPON YOUR HEART: DAILY REFLECTIONS ON SPIRITUAL CLASSICS

Large-quantity purchases or custom editions of this book are available at a discount from the publisher. For more information, contact the sales department at Augsburg Fortress, Publishers, 1-800-328-4648, or write to: Sales Director, Augsburg Fortress, Publishers, P.O. Box 1209, Minneapolis, MN 55440-1209.

Scripture passages, unless otherwise marked, are from the Revised Standard Version of the Bible, copyright © 1946, 1952, 1971, 1989 by the Division of Christian Education of the National Council of the Churches of Christ in the USA. Used by permission.

Cover design by Sarah Gioe
Cover art by Stock Illustration Source; interior art by PhotoDisc
Book design by Michelle L. N. Cook

Library of Congress Cataloging-in-Publication Data
These words upon your heart : daily reflections on spiritual classics / edited by Paul Ofstedal.
    p. cm.
Includes bibliographical references (p.).
ISBN 0-8066-4421-4 (alk. paper)
    1. Devotional calendars. I. Ofstedal, Paul, 1932–
BV4810 .T43 2001
242'.2—dc21   2001045904

The paper used in this publication meets the minimum requirements of American National Standard for Information Sciences—Permanence of Paper for Printed Library Materials, ANSI Z329.48-1984.

Manufactured in the U.S.A.   AF 9-4421

06   05   04   03   02   1   2   3   4   5   6   7   8   9   10

CONTENTS

FOREWORD BY BRADLEY P. HOLT

SPIRITUAL READING INVITES A RICH DIALOGUE. THE READER RESPONDS to the expressed thoughts of the writer, whether by feeling and thought alone or in writing, perhaps in a journal. This conversation at its best will change the reader's life, suddenly or gradually. Through this dialogue, the Holy Spirit will startle or nudge the reader into a new perspective and new behavior.

In *Take and Read: Spiritual Reading,* Eugene Peterson writes, "Spiritual reading, for most of us, requires either the recovery or acquisition of skills not in current repute: leisurely, repetitive, reflective reading. In this we are not reading primarily for information, but for companionship."

These Words Upon Your Heart introduces the reader to some of the most engaging companions in the history of Christian spirituality. At the same time it offers a bridge to them through the reflections of someone in our own time. What wonderful potentials for three-way conversations lie within these covers!

Christians think first of the Bible as spiritual reading, and this is right. The Bible contains all that we need for salvation. It tells the story of God's conversation with the people of Israel, and then God's Incarnation as one of us. It teaches that we are brought into communion with God by God's grace, not by our striving. (Striving may include reading, praying, writing, and other spiritual disciplines!) Our life of spiritual practice flows out from God's love for us.

But the Spirit is not limited to the Scripture in bearing fruitful messages to God's people. The millennia since the Bible was written have produced spiritual dialogues that reflect on the dialogues in Scripture. It is our privilege in this book to listen in on some of them. We may join the conversation and listen for the Spirit's nudges and surprises, too.

What the Bible does not claim to give us and cannot give us, is conversation with later disciples of Jesus down through the ages in their many cultural settings—women and men, early and recent, Asians, Africans, Europeans, Americans. We learn from one another. In the Gospel of John, Jesus is remarkably open to the future. He says, "The one who believes in me will also do the works that I do and, in fact, will do greater works than these, because I am going to the Father," and "The Advocate, the Holy Spirit, whom the Father will send in my name, will teach you everything" (John 14:12, 25). We are a network of reflection and action on the gospel message. Just as joining a discussion group on the Internet today can develop new friendships and new insights, so plugging in to this multicentury and multicultural conversation can do the same, but on a much wider scale.

How wide is your acquaintance with the "cloud of witnesses" (Hebrews: 12:1)? Does it go beyond ancient days up to our very own? This volume will provide you, the spiritual reader, with plenty of good material for dialogue. Take your time, use your God-given imagination, and the Spirit will both comfort and disturb you! For this is not just an intellectual exercise. Spiritual reading can touch not just the mind, but the whole person. That is why this book is called *These Words Upon Your Heart.*

—Bradley P. Holt, Ph.D.

author of *Thirsty for God* and *The Inward Pilgrimage*

PREFACE

THE FOLLOWING PAGES INTRODUCE YOU TO TWELVE OF THE finest spiritual writers from the Christian tradition, from Saint Augustine to Thomas Merton. (This book contains a selection of chapters from a longer work published in 1990, *Daily Readings from Spiritual Classics.*) Each classic writer is introduced by a brief biography. This is followed by ten devotional reflections by contemporary Christians responding to the words of this spiritual writer. We've also included a bibliography of the spiritual classics. It is only a start, but we hope it will whet your appetite for more from these and other Christian classics.

For further background on the Christian spiritual tradition you may wish to read Bernhard Christensen's book *The Inward Pilgrimage: An Introduction to Spiritual Classics* and Bradley P. Holt's *Thirsty for God: A Brief History of Christian Spirituality.*

My thanks to the contemporary writers who added their own reflections to the texts from the spiritual classics. Theirs has been a humbling task, requiring courage, entered with trepidation. It was also a labor of love. We are in their debt. I also thank the staff and members of First Lutheran Church in Williston, North Dakota, where I was pastor at the time, for their encouragement in this project.

I have dedicated this book to my beloved family as a combined guilt and love offering. The love hardly needs comment, but the guilt does. My intentions ever since I took a Christian classics course at Luther College were to acquaint my future family with these beacons of faith and wisdom. Too many years went by before I acted on those good intentions. Once more, it's "better late than never."

Throughout this volume, source references that relate directly to the classic author in question are keyed to the bibliography at the back of the book. As you read, you will note, following quoted material, both an author's last name and a year enclosed in parentheses. To find the source of the quote, refer to the bibliography at the back of the book. There the last name of the author in parentheses is listed alphabetically, followed by the rest of the source information.

May our reading herein be to the praise of his glory who made peace by the blood of his cross (Col. 1:20).

—Paul Ofstedal

x

AUGUSTINE

William Smith

AUGUSTINE (354–430) WAS BORN SOME 40 YEARS AFTER Christianity had become the acknowledged religion of the Roman Empire under Constantine. His birthplace was Numidia, a Roman province in North Africa.

His father, Patricus, reasonably well off, remained a pagan until shortly before death, when he was baptized. Augustine's mother, Monica, on the other hand, was a Christian of tremendous piety. As his mother prayed, Augustine dedicated his life to the service of Christ and the church. She made him a saint and his sanctity eventually resulted in her being canonized.

By the end of the fourth century the decadence that had afflicted Rome had spread to the northern African provinces, especially to the great port of Carthage, at whose university Augustine studied. He excelled there and soon became a highly regarded teacher of rhetoric. Then he transferred to Rome because he found Carthage students too turbulent. In Rome he could find an academic position that would lead to great status and power. There was yet another darker motive: he wanted to escape from the watchful eye of his mother, and indulge himself more freely.

In Rome he was appointed to the Chair of Rhetoric in Milan. This brought him in contact with the imperial court and, even more importantly, with the saintly Bishop Ambrose. Under Ambrose's influence Augustine began to study the Scriptures, noting particularly the spiritual meaning of Old Testament stories. This played an important part in his final deliverance from the heresy of Manicheism and his ultimate conversion, described in the *Confessions*. Augustine returned with Monica to North Africa, resolving to dedicate the remaining years of his life wholly to the service of Christ. But his gifts were too celebrated and precious for him to be left in peace.

He was forty-three years old when he became Bishop of Hippo. Thenceforth, he was endlessly involved in the responsibilities of his office and the often bitter controversies of his time. In the year 410, Rome had been sacked. Augustine was forced to turn to the question of the relation between earthly cities like Rome, which rise and fall, and the heavenly city, or city of God, which is everlasting. This question resulted in his great work, *The City of God*, in which he concluded that in Jesus Christ, the presence of God who has come to us in human form, we have a "window in the walls of time which looks out on to this Heavenly City."

WE ARE DRAWN TO PRAISE GOD

One of Augustine's greatest contributions to Christian literature is his book *Confessions*. With such an ambiguous title, one may ask, Is Augustine intending a confession of sin? Of faith? Or is this simply his autobiography? While all of these elements are found in *Confessions,* it is not Augustine's primary concern to reveal himself and his faith in God. The focus of *Confessions* is God! It is God who is before him and about whom he writes. The book starts with praise of God and ends with praise of creation—a creation that is good, created by a God who is wonderfully good. The heart of the book, then, is the confession of praise.

Why do we sing praises to God? Is it because we have a God before whom we tremble? "No!" says Augustine. It is something else. We must praise God out of our experiencing God's goodness, God's greatness, God's beauty. It is the expression of one's heart filled with the love of God (Rom. 5:5). The heart feels who this God is and is drawn to praise God. Praise is an inevitable expression of that awareness. So the book begins, *"Thou art great, O Lord, and greatly to be praised."* *

Augustine asserts that our God-given, inner beauty and our desire to praise God are no longer present in their original form. However, he sees "traces of the trinity" in the inner soul of each individual, just as he does when he views the beauty and grandeur of God's creation as a whole. Though darkened by original sin, wonderful attributes can be found in all people.

The book is centered in the praise of God who was there all along in Augustine's life, mysteriously guiding and directing him, and who, he was convinced, would continue to direct him in his very active life as long as he lived.

Can you think of times when you have been especially conscious of this desire to praise God in your life?

3

---

* *Quotations from Augustine throughout this chapter have been translated from Latin by the author. The sources are listed in the bibliography.*

WE ARE CREATED TO BE WITH GOD

"Since we are a part of your creation, we wish to praise you. The thought of you stirs us so deeply that we cannot be content unless we praise you, because you made us to be with you and our hearts are restless until they rest in you."

Here is one of the fundamental "traces of the trinity" for Augustine. We are created to be with God. We might say that no person is really human without God, according to Augustine. Without God, the humanity of that person is, if not lost, at least diminished. Our only proper place is to be with God.

Augustine would claim that a restlessness is "built into" every human being, that there is an awareness, at some level in every person, that one has no real being, no true existence without God. He prays: "O God, I should have no being at all unless you were in me, or rather I should not be unless I had being in you." Augustine's own restless yearning, his pining for this loving, unchangeable God, is expressed in this prayer: *"You are never new, never old, and yet all things have new life from you. . . . Who will grant me to rest content in you? To whom shall I turn for the gift of your coming into my heart and filling it to the brim so that I might forget all the wrong I have done and embrace you alone, my only source of good."*

How has this "inner restlessness" been expressed in your life? Can you reflect on those moments when you have been most aware of "yearning and pining" for God to come into your heart and fill it to the brim with his loving presence?

IN LOVE GOD CREATES AND SUSTAINS

Augustine finds hints or evidence of the presence of God, "traces of the trinity," from the very beginning of his life. He sees them in his mother's sacrificial love, the love of one who pointed him to the first ray of divine light, the light which is Jesus Christ.

"The comfort of my mother's milk maintained my life. Yet neither did my mother nor my nurses fill their own breasts, but you, O Lord, did so, and afforded nourishment fit for my infancy, even according to your planning and riches which are arranged even to the lowest order of things."

From his mother Monica's little lamp of faith he saw the first light of God, the first light of Jesus Christ, the first light of the Holy Spirit. We, also, who at the beginning of our existence have all these infant needs can reflect later (as Augustine did) with deep warmth and gratitude for God's love coming to us through a mother's love. Some of us, however, may bear deep scars, spiritually as well as emotionally, because we were deprived of such love.

For Augustine, evidence of the presence of God could be seen, not only in the first work of divine love by which God created him and brought him into this world, but also in that next work of God's love in which he was sustained by the comfort of his mother's milk.

What experiences do you recall from your early life that have helped you see God's work of divine love in creating and sustaining you?

THE NAME OF JESUS CHRIST

Augustine, in his years of higher learning, became a very zealous student. During this time another "trace of the trinity," an indication of God's continued activity in his life, occurred in his study of a book by Cicero. It was called the *Hortensius* (*hortensius* means "gardener"). This book contained an invitation to a meaningful life. It was not propaganda for a special school of philosophy, but a call to a lifelong search for true wisdom. Augustine characterizes the influence of the book this way: "*. . . that book changed my feelings and changed my prayers to you, O Lord. It altered my wishes and my desires. All former empty hopes lost significance for me, and I was yearning with incredible ardor of heart after the immortality of wisdom. I began to rise up so that I might turn to you, O God. . . . How did I burn then, my God, how did I burn to flee from earthly delights to you. Yet, I was unaware of what you were doing with me. For wisdom dwells with you.*"

The most remarkable thing in all of Augustine's experience in reading *Hortensius* was how he found himself missing the name of Christ. Didn't he know that Cicero lived before the birth of Jesus? Clearly, this work was written before the Christian era. Yet he says: "*The only thing to dim my ardor was the fact that the name of Christ was not there, for this name, by your mercy, O Lord, this name of my Savior, your son, my youthful heart had drunk in piously with my mother's milk and, until that time, had retained it in its depth; whatever lacked this name could not completely win me, however well expressed and polished and true appearing.*"

In Augustine's soul the presence of God was planted so deeply that it could not be uprooted or eliminated. Jesus Christ had written his name indelibly on Augustine's soul through the loving hands of his mother, Monica. So much so, that there was in him an inward necessity to have God as his heavenly Father, and Jesus Christ as his Savior.

How has that inward necessity to have God as your heavenly Father and Jesus Christ as your Savior been formed in you?

GOD SPEAKS TO US

It is obvious that a "trace of the trinity" in Augustine's pilgrimage of faith would be his conversion experience in the garden described in Book 8. This episode is often overly dramatized. This was not as cataclysmic an event for Augustine as is often portrayed. It was, rather, the culmination of God's working in him over a long period of time. It was a time when he was inwardly running in circles, coming closer to recognizing that he had to do something drastic about his life. Relief finally came when God had his way with Augustine. He knew that he could not live without Christ any longer. All his rational arguments against faith in Christ had evaporated.

Compare this scene with Augustine's last conversation with his mother, Monica, found in Book 9. The two of them contemplate the divine glory of eternal life after death, that which "eye has not seen, nor ear heard, nor entered into one's heart." This transcendent moment for Augustine sheds light on all past experiences of God's presence in his life from infancy to the present. In this moment both he and Monica were in a state of profound yearning to reach "with the mouth of the heart those mountains and streams flowing above," so that they might reflect on those great things according to their capacity. He and his mother came to the conclusion that the highest point of human pleasure is not worth comparing to the awareness of that eternal life of God's divine presence, which they had experienced in the silence of the soul.

This experience offered Augustine an awareness that, by God's grace, the heavenly world and our earthly world are joined. This perception filled Augustine with an inward blessedness and strength, knowing that we humans are not left alone on earth in this life.

Because of this experience Augustine was able to say: "We are assured of our possession of these three things: eternal life, eternal truth, and eternal love, not on the testimony of others, but by our own consciousness of their presence and because we see it with our most truthful interior vision."

RESIDENT ALIENS

The basic trait in the "resident alien," as Augustine writes in his great work *The City of God,* is seeing one's true citizenship in the invisible city of God. This means a growing awareness for the believer that one lives out the whole of one's life here on earth as a temporary resident. For Augustine, however, this implies that we, as Christians, must accept an intimate dependence on the community around us; we must realize that our common life was created by people like ourselves, to achieve some "good" that we are glad to share with them, to improve some situation, to avoid some greater evil; we must be genuinely grateful for the favorable conditions that it provides. However, Augustine expected that as "resident aliens" Christians would always be aware of the tenacity of those links that bind us to the world.

But we need to remember in these reflections, based mainly on *The City of God,* that, far from being a book about flight from the world, it is a book whose recurrent theme is "our business within this common mortal life." It is a book about being other-worldly while living in this world.

If you were asked, as a Christian, what it meant to you to be "in the world but not of the world," what would you say? Have there been times when an awareness of "being other-worldly in this world" has been most real for you as a Christian? How did that awareness come about? What effect did this have on you inwardly?

LIVING AS RESIDENT ALIENS

Should the Christian be like everyone else, totally involved in the affairs of the world and totally immersed in its passions and pursuits? Should the aims of the Christian include the search for enjoyment of life, for possessions, for high position and status in society? Or should the Christian aspire to something even higher, having some distance and detachment from these other aims and desires, without denying their relative value? These are the questions that Augustine poses in *The City of God*.

Augustine turned to the Scriptures for help in answering these questions: "I beseech you as aliens and exiles to abstain from the passions of the flesh that wage war against your soul. Maintain good conduct among the Gentiles, so that in case they speak against you as wrongdoers, they may see your deeds and glorify God on the day of visitation" (1 Pet. 2:11–12). Here the Christian is characterized as not really being a citizen of this world, but in some way an alien. The Christian is a citizen of another country, a citizen with full rights of citizenship there. The writer to the Ephesians says, "So then you are no longer strangers and sojourners, but you are fellow citizens with the saints and members of the household of God, built upon the foundation of the apostles and prophets, Christ Jesus himself being the cornerstone" (Eph. 2:19–20).

This attitude, which is developed and emphasized by Augustine, was a basic orientation of the early Christian. Now, a question for you in these reflections on the Christian as "resident alien": How might such an attitude in our lives, as modern Christians, not only offer us help in recovering from inward conflicts, psychic distortions and sickness, but lead us toward a greater sense of the presence of Christ in our lives?

ORDER IN ME MY LOVE

The soul of the "resident alien" is in permanent tension between two powers pulling the Christian inwardly in opposite directions. Augustine speaks of these powers as "two loves." The two cities, the heavenly and earthly, are founded by these two loves. The one is the love of oneself (characteristic of the earthly city). This love of oneself goes so far as to disregard God. The heavenly love, on the contrary, goes so far in loving God as to forget oneself. The one glories in oneself. The other glories in God. The one seeks glory from other persons. But the great glory of the other is God who is giving witness of his forgiving love in one's conscience. The one loves ruling, dominating, and subduing. The other, in contrast, seeks to serve another in love. The one has delight in its own strength. The other has God as its strength.

Augustine believed that there is a deep love for God hidden within the heart of every believer. This highest, most sublime love for God does not imply for Augustine, however, that such a love swallows up all other lesser loves. Rather, he saw all these other loves—love of one's betrothed, love of spouse, family, friends, love of beauty, art, music, nature—as flowing out of this love for God. Augustine would ask us, as modern "resident alien" Christians, to maintain our identity, not by withdrawal from this "earthly city," but by something far more difficult, by maintaining a firm and balanced perspective on the whole range of loves of which we are capable in our present state. He would ask us, as members of Christ's body of believers, his church, inhabitants of the City of God—now by faith, and in the life to come, by sight—to join him in a simple prayer he repeatedly prayed: "Order in me my love."

When would you find (or perhaps have already found) words like these most helpful and vital for you to pray in your own Christian life?

UNCEASING PRAYER

How do we become aware of the "resident alien" consciousness in our lives as Christians? Augustine replies, *"Give me one who longs, who hungers, who is a thirsty pilgrim in this wilderness, sighing for the springs of the eternal City: give me such a person; that one will know what I mean."* He reminds us that God, who sees in secret and knows our hearts, is aware of these hidden groanings within us and will reward us (cf. Matt. 6:6). How will God reward us? For one thing, we can become aware that this very longing, this inner yearning, this sighing within, is our praying; and if this longing continues, our praying is continual too.

"It was not for nothing," says Augustine, *"that the apostle Paul said, 'Pray without ceasing' (1 Thess. 5:17). Can we unceasingly bend our knees, bow down our bodies, or uplift our hands that the apostle should tell us to 'pray without ceasing'? No, if it is thus he bids us pray, I do not think we can do so without ceasing. There is another way of praying, interior and unbroken, and that is the way of longing, of desire. Whatever else you are doing, if you long for that City, that eternal homeland, you are not ceasing to pray. If you do not want to cease praying, do not cease longing. Your unceasing desire is your unceasing prayer."*

Augustine was concerned that this longing not be allowed to grow cold through the preoccupation of our everyday life. He would encourage us "resident alien" believers to find ways of stirring up this longing at "certain fixed times so that it may be brought to a glow." Would it not be of comfort for you to believe that your very yearning for God's peace, your sighing within to know more fully of God's forgiving love, and your desire to fix your eyes more firmly on the eternal city of God—that this longing and desire within you is an expression of your unceasing prayer?

OUR LOVE FOR GOD

We can see that the heart of Augustine's understanding of the "resident alien" consciousness of the Christian is expressed in "longing for the vision of God." *"Nothing that God can promise is of any worth apart from God Himself. What is all the earth, the sea, the sky, the stars . . . the hosts of angels? For the creator of them all I thirst, for Him I hunger. . . ."* Augustine refers to this "longing for the vision of God" at times as "pure love" by which he means loving God for God's own sake. *"The heart is not pure,"* he says, *"if it worships God for a reward. What then? Shall we have no reward for the worship of God? Assuredly we shall, but it will be God Himself whom we worship: His own self will be our reward, in that we shall see Him as He is. . . . If you worship God who freely wrought your undeserved redemption, if when you consider God's goodness toward you, your heart sighs and is restless with longing for God; then seek not from God anything outside God, God Himself suffices you."*

Augustine would try to illustrate this by pointing out that in serious illness we long for health, but when restoration of health comes, that longing is dispatched. In a similar way when we, as believers, attain the perfect health, which is life eternal in the City of God, "we shall feel need no longer, and therein will be our happiness. For we shall be filled with our God, who Himself will be to us all that our longings make us count most desirable here."

But now Augustine would ask about my daily pilgrimage as a "resident alien" Christian when the fulfillment is not yet; what is my good here and now? His answer: *"So long as you are not yet fast joined to God, set there your hope . . . cleave to God in hope. And here (in this life) setting your hope in God, what will you have to do? What will be your work, but to praise Him you love and to get others to share your love of Him?"*

Could you reflect on any persons or events in your life that have edified and strengthened you in faith? Can you think of times when you've shared your love for God with other people?

St. Francis of Assisi

Herbert Brokering

He was born into the family of a rich cloth merchant in a small Italian town in the Umbrian Valley. Pietro Bernardoni and his French wife, the Lady of Pica, baptized their son Giovanni. Later his wealthy father changed the name to Francesco, and we now know him as St. Francis of Assisi (1182–1226). He grew up a spoiled son, full of humor, generosity, wit, charm. He was a raucous, musical, sensual troubadour, a prodigal.

In the act of becoming a knight at age twenty-two, he forsook the glamour of sword, shield, and death. A new light came into him, the light and sight of a child. This new eye for all life would never leave him. He heard voices and saw visions that led into a desert journey. Francis was listening to God.

From a crucifix he heard a voice commanding him to repair a nearby chapel on the verge of ruin. The priest would not accept the prodigal money which was his father's, so Francesco turned to begging. With stones received through begging, he rebuilt the church.

Francesco was mocked, returned what he had to his father, and stripped himself of all possessions. In rags he became a new person. The transformation was a ritual of baptism. Pietro Bernardoni is no longer his father; Francesco's Father is in heaven. He did not give a tithe: he gave everything. He was a fool but not foolhardy. He was streetwise and then memorized songs of red-winged blackbirds. His earthly father was a cloth merchant, but his Father in heaven made him a man of the cloth—it was tattered and torn, and it was often a towel.

SISTER EARTH

Be praised, my Lord, for our sister Mother Earth,
Who sustains and guides us,
and brings forth fruits of many kinds,
with many colored flowers of grass.
—Cornelia 1985

The earth is kind. Gardens, meadows, woodlands gladly give more than we need. Mother earth is Sister, partner in the family. We cheer when the buds burst; we thank for the fruit we eat. The one who gives us what we need is part of our family. Mother earth is partner, Sister.

Earth is a pantry. We have a right to the bounty of all the earth. We need the lap and arms and warmth of Sister Mother Earth. Earth is kinder than a friend; earth is Sister.

Earth is a minister to the human spirit. She uses all her gifts and forms. Earth can be Mother and Sister in long night watches. In a storm she can make strangers one close family. Rain can make thankless people praise. We are all in the mercy of Sister Earth. She is God's full-time minister.

St. Francis spoke lovingly of earth. He was earth's brother. We are to greet earth with dignity and call her by her endearing name. We find in earth our daily life and food. We find in earth our work and play and all mysteries. We find in her an abundance.

Dear mother earth, who day by day
Unfolds rich blessings on our way,
Oh, praise [God]! Alleluia!
The fruits and flow'rs that verdant grow,
Let them his praise abundant show.
Oh, praise [God]!
—LBW 527

"The earth is the Lord's and the fullness thereof, the world and those who dwell therein" (Ps. 24:1).

14

SISTER WATER

Be praised, my Lord, for Sister Water,
most useful is she, and humble,
and precious and chaste.
—Cornelia 1985

 raise the Lord for water says St. Francis. By nature water is precious and chaste. For St. Francis all water was inspired. Jesus was washed in water, so all water belongs to Christ. In the same way, all nature is God's nature. Francis had no more possessions than the lowest creation. So he loved all things, and the lowliest of all loved him in return. Francis knew the water loved him.

There is nothing water will not wash clean. There is no thirst it will not heal. Water is the drink for rich and poor. The rose garden in Washington, D.C., and your lawn need the same water. Queens, prisoners, and actors wash in one water. Water and towel are a sign of forgiveness. Jesus amazed his disciples in the Upper Room with Sister Water and the towel.

Water is a common character in spiritual dramas. God's people still have favorite water holes, cups, fountains, lakes. All know a struggling creek, rampaging river, collapsed cistern, and dry well. Picture water stories of salvation. Through water God saves the world and family of Noah, the nation of Israel, the prophet Jonah, the army of Gideon, the woman in Samaria. Sister Water is a main character in Scriptures and church history.

15

Let water be the sacred sign
That we must die each day
To rise again by his design
As foll'wers of his way
—LBW 195

"*Have you entered into the springs of the sea, or walked in the recesses of the deep?*" (Job 38:16).

YOURS IS THE PRAISE

Most High, mighty and good Lord,
Yours is the praise, the glory, the honor
and all benediction.
To you alone, Most High, do they belong,
and no one is fit even to mention your name.
—Cornelia 1985

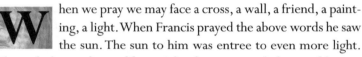

When we pray we may face a cross, a wall, a friend, a painting, a light. When Francis prayed the above words he saw the sun. The sun to him was entree to even more light. Through the sun he could see sights for praise and glory and honor.

When we pray we travel through insight. In secret, in silence, and while transfixed our thoughts go far and fast and close. The goal of prayer is God. The depth or height of prayer is to praise.

Prayer is an astonishing mode of speaking. Though simple it is not commonplace. It is a surprise that we may know and speak the name of God. Francis knew what it meant to revel. What he did in prayer some saw as dance and clown. He never took the joy away from others, but saw delight and celebration as pointing to the Most High.

Most High: what a name for God. And if Most High, then Most Low, Most Deep, Most Wide, Most Far, Most Near. Nothing is too exaggerated. Nothing is too humble. Nothing is too little. Nothing is too much. We belong to the one Most High.

Oh, that I had a thousand voices
To praise my God with thousand tongues!
My heart, which in the Lord rejoices,
Would then proclaim in grateful songs
To all, wherever I might be,
What great things God has done for me.
—LBW 560

"And the city has no need for sun or moon to shine upon it, for the glory of
God is its light, and its lamp is the Lamb" (Rev. 21:23).

BROTHER WIND

Be praised, my Lord, for Brother Wind,
and for the air, for cloudy, fair,
and every kind of weather,
through which you give your creatures sustenance.
—Cornelia 1985

There are those who, like St. Francis, bless the wind: the tailwind that makes the flight on time, the wind that brings needed rain, and the wind to cool heat at dusk.

Some watch clouds and praise God for Brother Wind. There is a country church high on a single hill where often blows a high wind. Some hang on to their hats and hurry through the door. Some face the wind and revel in it thankfully. Wind is their Brother.

Wind is a synonym for breath. When runners need a second wind they rejoice in the gift. When we need spirit, Brother Wind is there. We wait for the wind through the cry of newborn. Handel's "Messiah" always features a chorus of wind, harmonies learned from the wind in woods.

Brother Wind leads us by scent to roses, tree blossoms, and oceans. By the wind the dog can smell home. By the wind we know places, we smell that dinner is ready and candles are lit.

The wind and breath of God lives in us. There is spirit and breath as when God spoke to Ezekiel saying that the dry bones would live when God put his breath in them. When we travel believing, we journey far and high with Brother Wind. We hear the Spirit speaking to us, calling us. We listen for constant songs of praise.

O rushing wind and breezes soft,
O clouds that ride the winds aloft:
Oh, praise him! Alleluia!
—*LBW* 527

"Let everything that breathes praise the Lord! Praise the Lord!"
(Ps. 150:6).

LOVE

Be praised, my Lord,
for those who grant pardon
for love of you,
and endure infirmity and tribulation.
—Cornelia 1985

These words were always in St. Francis's Friday prayer. Friday was the day to ask pardon, because on that one Friday they did not pardon him who pardoned them all. They did not love him, who said: "Forgive them; for they know not what they do" (Luke 23:34).

There is a shout of pardon to be heard; the pardon we seek we already have. We come to know the great love St. Francis knew. Because we are loved we seek more love and will find it. There is a way to love Christ that makes others feel loved. In our devotion for Christ we learn to be devoted to each other.

Francis knew the key to love. He knew the joy love brings. He knew the simple acts of being loved. We know how direct love must be. Love surrounds and is within. Love begets love. Love begat creation. Love overwhelms. God knows all about love.

God leads us to the thirsty, the lonely, the imprisoned, and the enemy. And when we arrive, God's work of reconciliation has already begun. God always leads us into love.

O Love that will not let me go,
I rest my weary soul in thee;
I give thee back the life I owe,
That in thine ocean depths its flow
May richer, fuller be.
—*LBW* 324

"This is my commandment, that you love one another as I have loved you. Greater love has no man than this, that a man lay down his life for his friends" (John 15:12–13).

THE WEALTH

You are all the wealth one can desire.
You are beauty. You are gentleness.
You are our protector.
—Cornelia 1985

The sun had not yet risen. Morning was still behind the horizon. Francis trusted God when there was little to see. Where is the wealth of the Lord? We may need to close our eyes to see this bounty. We may need to fold our hands, be alone, and feel pangs of hunger to know God's wealth. The Lord is the wealth.

Francis was raised in the house of a clothier, a merchant of fine cloth. Yet there was a beauty he found to be greater than fine linen: it was in all that Christ had touched or seen. What Christ had set his eyes on turned to beauty, Francis learned.

Francis names the Lord "Wealth." There is no greater asset, than the "Wealth." Everything from shadows to seasons to spirits to reasons has worth. We are totally immersed in wealth. What is most essential for life cannot be manufactured. It can be discovered. Great need can take us to great wealth quickly.

It is happening now. At this moment we can desire any wealth, any beauty, any protection. The wealth Francis is describing is the Lord. Prayer takes us into this wealth. Closing our eyes we can be there. Folding or reaching our arms we can be there. Saying one word we can be there in the middle of the wealth.

For the joy of ear and eye,
For the heart and mind's delight,
For the mystic harmony
Linking sense to sound and sight:
Christ, our Lord, to you we raise
This our sacrifice of praise
—LBW 561

"I will not leave you desolate; I will come to you" (John 14:18).

BLESSED SUN

Be praised, my Lord, for all your creatures,
in the first place for Blessed Sun,
who gives us the day
and enlightens us through you,
beautiful and radiant,
giving witness to you, Most High.
—Cornelia 1985

In first place of all things created for Francis was Blessed Sun. "Let there be light" is the first stanza of the hymn in Genesis. He could shout "Amen" to a beam of light. Through Blessed Sun God gives us day. So we have long horizons, deep vistas, sharp shadows. Blessed Sun is a sign of many ways to see.

Blessed Sun is our mentor. We too want to radiate, be enlightened, shine. We too want to grow, ripen, bloom, enliven. We like the feeling of seeing some glory.

There is a higher light than the sun. It has more brightness, radiance, and beauty than a bright day. There is a sight so bright that in its sudden moments we stammer with angels to exclaim.

Higher than Blessed Sun is the Most High. All day, all light, all enlightenment is a witness. To follow all forms of sun and light leads us to the Most High. All light is a spotlight on the Most High.

O Jesus, shine around us, With radiance of your grace;
O Jesus, turn upon us, The brightness of your face.
We need no star to guide us, As on our way we press,
If you will light our pathway, O Sun of righteousness.
—*LBW 77*

"Lord, now lettest thou thy servant depart in peace, according to thy word;
for mine eyes have seen thy salvation" (Luke 2:29–30).

PARDON ME

Be praised, my Lord,
for those who grant pardon
for love of you,
and endure infirmity and tribulation.
—Cornelia 1985

Francis knew pardon. At Francis's worst times Christ was in best form, granting pardon. And during our worst times, Christ is with the downcast and the outcast, for Christ became the outcast.

Christ came to us to be human. The frown of God is gone. Curtains are torn in two. Partitions are abolished. God's rainbow shouts one will: Pardon. All is changed now because Christ hung on the unpardonable shape, the cross.

Life can go on without our perishing. We can submit to tribulation. We can carry the cross. There is in us a life and love of Christ. It is in us and around us. Love goes before and after.

The greatest of all we possess is love. We are born into love; it is stronger than all else. Love converts water into wine, an acorn into a lumber yard, a convict into a disciple, a thief into a friend, a stumbling block into a cornerstone.

"Forgive our sins as we forgive," You taught us, Lord, to pray:
But you alone can grant us grace, To live the words we say.

Lord, cleanse the depths within our souls, And bid resentment cease;
Then, bound to all in bonds of love, Our lives will spread your peace.
—*LBW* 307

"For the commandments . . . are summed up in this sentence, 'You shall love your neighbor as yourself'" (Rom. 13:9).

THE DREAM

Lord, make me an instrument of your peace.
Where there is hatred, let me sow love,
Where there is injury, pardon,
Where there is darkness, light,
Where there is despair, hope
And where there is sadness, joy.
—Bodo 1972

T he sight of Francis, a poor beggar in the palace of the Turkish sultan, was a study of contrasts. He'd come to tell his majesty about Jesus. He'd come to tell of the peace he'd found along life's way. His words flowed like a rich wine.

The sultan heard that the poor beggar from Assisi sought to balance the world's hatred. Francis told him not what the sultan wanted to hear, but the truth. This poem of peace lays paradoxes upon the great scale of justice. Francis does not ask to destroy despair, darkness, injury, or hatred. Where there is hatred, he would sow love.

We are going somewhere. This dream is more than images inside us. It is evident; the dream lives; people hear it in our words and see our eyes on fire. It is a road we will not leave. It is a long journey to tents of sultans and places of danger. We share a dream of peace, and then we go home.

Grant peace, we pray, in mercy, Lord;
Peace in our time, oh, send us!
For there is none on earth but you,
None other to defend us.
You only, Lord, can fight for us. Amen
—*LBW* 417

"*And above all these put on love, which binds everything together in perfect harmony. And let the peace of Christ rule in your hearts, to which indeed you were called in the one body. And be thankful*"(Col. 3:14–15).

JESUS

O Lord, I beg of you two graces before I die—
to experience personally and in all possible fullness
the pains of your bitter Passion,
and to feel for you the same love
that moved you to sacrifice yourself for us.
—Bodo 1984

For everything in Francis's life Jesus was in the center. It was in the cave that he first met Jesus. In the cave he found a hidden center of himself. Christ helped him into that inner place for strength and peace.

He embraced the Christ found in the center of the publicans and sinners. There was a stigma of Jesus that Francis wanted; he believed the markings of Jesus would be his surest sign of unity.

The Jesus whom Francis knew is the one who did not grab equality with God, and who took on the nature of a slave. He had no regular place to lie down, and died in a robe that was not his own.

In his last days, friends carried Francis down to the valley of the little church, St. Mary of the Angels. He lay there stripped of his habit on the cold floor with the thought and hope to die naked as Christ. He would not be hoisted on the cross as Christ had been. He would die lying on cold stone, with the wound in his side.

There is something in this dream that is ours. For Francis, as for us, Jesus is the center. Jesus is the beginning, and Jesus is the end. In death we come full circle. The one who shared the open grave in our baptism, is the one who says: "It is I!" at the end.

Jesus, priceless treasure, Source of purest pleasure,
Truest friend to me: Ah, how long I've panted,
And my heart has fainted, Thirsting, Lord, for Thee.
—LBW 458

"He said to them, 'But who do you say that I am?' Simon Peter replied, 'You are the Christ, the Son of the living God'" (Matt. 16:15–16).

JULIAN OF NORWICH

Stephanie Frey

IF ONE IS IN SEARCH OF PRECISE BIOGRAPHICAL DATA ABOUT the woman named Julian, whose legacy to us is her manuscript "Revelations of Divine Love," there is little to be found. According to the manuscript itself, Julian of Norwich was a woman who lived during the fourteenth century and made her home in Norwich, England. Most manuscripts give a date of May 13, 1373, her 30th year of life, as the occasion upon which she experienced the set of visions recorded in her book. Julian was quite ill when the visions occurred, so ill that her priest had been sent to bring her a crucifix on which to gaze. The visions she received are all centered around the image of Christ on the cross.

At some point, Julian became an anchoress, and entered a monastic cell that was part of the Church of St. Julian at Norwich. As was customary she took the name of the patron saint of the anchorhold. She remained in the anchorhold at Norwich until the time of her death, thought to be between 1416 and 1419 A.D.

The contextual setting of her life is of great importance, even though there are few biographical details known. Julian lived during the time of the Hundred Years War, under the reign of Edward III. This was a time of decline in both church and state. Along with that, the bubonic plague was sweeping the countryside—and death was all around her. Some scholars speculate that because of the high death rate, and the fact that many children were growing up without their mothers, Julian might have been prompted to develop her well-known image of Jesus as our Mother. She herself may have longed for mothering, and without a living mother of her own may have sought that particularly in her Lord.

Julian's writings are of import yet today for several reasons: they give us a sharp view of the medieval mind and theological perspective, they present to us a fine record of an individual's personal and profound experience of God, and they can draw us into an understanding of the lifegiving nature of such deep prayer as this. While it may be that some of Julian's observations would suffer today under a careful doctrinal examination, her writing can nevertheless prompt us to affirm our own creeds, to live in her world for a while, and to consider the awesome majesty of God's great love for all of humankind.

PASSION FOR CHRIST

". . . I thought I had already had some experience of the passion of Christ, but by his grace I wanted still more. I wanted to be actually there with Mary Magdalene and the Other who loved him, and with my own eyes to see and know more of the physical suffering of our Savior, and the compassion of our Lady and of those who were there and then were loving him truly and watching his pains. I would be one of them and suffer with them . . ." (Julian 1966).

There is hardly a believer who has not at some time wondered just what it would have been like to have been in a crowd that heard Jesus teach and saw him heal, or to have been one of the disciples at that Last Supper, or among the women who stood at the cross and then made their way in the early morning darkness to the empty tomb. The gospel story is so compelling, and draws us so close to itself, that we long for a way of knowing more nearly what the passion of Christ was like. As with Julian, there may be in us, especially during Lent and Holy Week, that desire actually to have been there.

Try as we might, we will not have the experience of being with Jesus in the flesh, nor will most of us have the visions of Julian as she lay sick and near death in the fourteenth century. But the lively Word of God, read and proclaimed, tells us that the Holy Spirit, working faith in us, will draw us near to God, near to the heart of the gospel. God has promised to create and nourish faith in us—and to give us the gifts of the Spirit, which include understanding. In that way we can begin to have understanding of what Christ's passion was, because we will know that it was for the love of us that it took place. To know that and have confidence in that is a great gift.

God of all mercy, work faith in us. Give us hearts of compassion and eyes to see with clarity, that through the accounts of your passion we may come to understand your unending love for us. Amen

RESTING IN GOD

"God is the True Rest who wants to be known. God finds pleasure in being our true resting place" (Doyle 1983).

How often people speak of the frantic pace of daily life in our time, the timeclocks of the workplace and the various clocks of family life. There are school schedules, work schedules, sports schedules, church schedules. The times given over to silence for meditation during Sunday worship are brief, as we feel the edginess of people for whom silence is foreign and perhaps even fearsome. How do we learn to rest? To rest from our daily schedules and even more important, to rest in God? Augustine knew the problem well: "My heart is restless until it rests in thee."

You and I belong to a God who rests: "And on the seventh day God finished his work which he had done, and he rested on the seventh day from all his work which he had done. So God blessed the seventh day and hallowed it, because on it God rested from all his work which he had done in creation" (Gen. 2:2–3).

And we have a Savior who invites us to rest: "Come to me, all who labor and are heavy laden, and I will give you rest. Take my yoke upon you, and learn from me; for I am gentle and lowly in heart, and you will find rest for your souls. For my yoke is easy, and my burden is light" (Matt. 11:28–30).

God is the one who promises to fill us and refresh us in those times of spiritual dryness. This God will be there in the silence of our rest. This God beckons us not to fear. This God "wants to be known," and is the one we can trust to cradle us in the everlasting arms, where there is true peace and rest.

O God, you rested when you were finished with this marvelous creation which gives us sustenance as well as delight in its mystery and beauty. You invite us now to rest from our work, and find a resting place in you. Help us quiet ourselves, and let the silence be filled with your promise and your peace, so we might be refreshed by you and your gospel of life. Amen

You Will Not Be Overcome

"God did not say:'You will not be tempested.You will not labor hard.You will not be troubled.' But God did say:'You will not be overcome'"(Doyle 1983).

I t does not take long in life for a person to encounter a situation in which they ask the question, "Why me?" The often unspoken part of that question is, "Why me?—I'm a Christian! What have I done to deserve this?"

In our day, there are those who preach the "victorious" Christian life—and who paint that life as a one lived perpetually on the mountaintop, on the crest of a wave, or on the "sunny side of the street." But the victory in the Christian life is a victory over death—not over the fact that we still live between the times of Christ's life on earth and his coming again.

Instead, our life as baptized people of God propels us directly into this "between-the-times" world in which we live. There is no need to seek out suffering, for it will come in one way, shape, or form to every person who has a heartbeat. We would be naive to think that the Christian life is free of such tyrannies.

Paul writes: "But we have this treasure in earthen vessels, to show that the transcendent power belongs to God and not to us. We are afflicted in every way, but not crushed; perplexed, but not driven to despair; persecuted, but not forsaken; struck down, but not destroyed; always carrying in the body the death of Jesus, so that the life of Jesus may also be manifested in our bodies" (2 Cor. 4:7–10).

In the face of suffering we still have hope, because God has loved us and gone even to the cross for us. We will not be overcome. We have the freedom to sing the song of others who have striven to throw off the chains of oppression: "We shall overcome. . . . Deep in my heart, I do believe, we shall overcome one day."

Almighty God, you have given me a treasure in earthen vessels: the undying hope we have in the gospel of Jesus. Carry us through the sufferings of this life, and give us a vision of a day when death and war and injustice will be no more. Amen

THE PAIN OF SIN

"But I did not see sin. I believe it has no substance or real existence. It can only be known by the pain it causes. This pain is something, as I see it, which lasts but a while. It purges us and makes us know ourselves, so that we ask for mercy" (Julian 1966).

It is striking how many times the effects of sin and wrong-doing are felt physically. Julian writes, "Sin . . . can only be known by the pain it causes." How easily the effects of sin can be felt in our own discomfort and wrongdoing, and in the emotional pain or "dis-ease" wreaked upon those whose lives are touched by that sin. Perhaps the physical discomfort we experience in such times is itself part of God's judgment in that moment. Perhaps it does serve, as Julian contends, to help us know our need and ask for forgiveness.

Julian goes on to say: *"The passion of our Lord is our comfort against all this—for such is his blessed will. Because of his tender love for those who are to be saved our good Lord comforts us at once and sweetly as if to say . . . 'All will be well, and all will be well and every manner of thing will be well'"* (Doyle 1983).

Julian's confident words that all will be well find an echo in the psalm: "The Lord is merciful and gracious, slow to anger and abounding in steadfast love. He will not always chide, nor will he keep his anger for ever. He does not deal with us according to our sins, nor requite us according to our iniquities. For as the heavens are high above the earth, so great is his steadfast love toward those who fear him; as far as the east is from the west, so far does he remove our transgressions from us" (Ps. 103:8–12).

Gracious and loving God, we rejoice that you look with compassion and tenderness upon our sin. We ask your forgiveness for all that has been hurtful to the neighbor, and pray that you will continue to work your way within us, to bring us to faith and new life. Amen

OUR FAITH IS A LIGHT

"Our faith is a light. . . . Because of the light we live; because of the night we suffer and grieve. . . .When we are done with grief our eyes will be suddenly enlightened, and in the shining brightness of the light we shall see perfectly. For our light is none other than God our Maker, and the Holy Spirit, in our Savior, Christ Jesus" (Julian 1966).

Julian well understands that faith in God brings light to our lives. If faith is light, it is born of the light of Christ who overcame the darkness of our world by being born in a stinking stable in a backwater town like Bethlehem. If faith is light, it is born of the light of Christ who overcame the darkness of our world by being raised to life after three days in the grave. It is as if all of God's story through the ages rushes back and forth from dark to light.

God our Creator spoke a creative word over the chaos, and fashioned from that great darkness both day and night. That old scoundrel Jacob wrestled in the night with an unknown stranger— and by morning's light realized that it was God with whom he had wrestled. The people of Israel traveled both by day and night, and God lit their way at night with a great pillar of fire. The psalmist looked for day from the pit of night when his couch was filled with tears. And Good Friday was as dark as dark could be when Jesus hung on the cross. It wasn't until Easter morning that the glorious light of the resurrection filled that burial garden.

You and I move from darkness to light and back again countless times in our lives. Even in the darkest of times, the faith God is working to create in us brings light to the darkness. God has promised that even a "dimly burning wick he will not quench" (Isa. 42:3). God grants grace sufficient for our needs, and gives us the faith we need to walk the baptismal journey of our lives.

Enlighten our darkness, O God, and make the light of your gospel shine among us. Sustain our faith so it can give light to our days. Carry us through the various darknesses of our lives, so we may enter your light at life's end. Amen

GOD NEVER BEGAN TO LOVE US

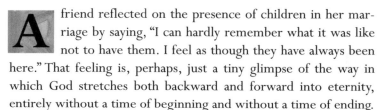

"I saw that God never began to love us. For just as we will be in everlasting joy (all God's creation is destined for this) so also we have always been in God's foreknowledge, known and loved from without beginning"(Doyle 1983).

A friend reflected on the presence of children in her marriage by saying, "I can hardly remember what it was like not to have them. I feel as though they have always been here." That feeling is, perhaps, just a tiny glimpse of the way in which God stretches both backward and forward into eternity, entirely without a time of beginning and without a time of ending.

Even more mystifying is the notion that we ourselves have been known and chosen by God from before we were a "twinkling in the Father's eye." How can we, who have two parents who gave us life, and birth certificates that note the hour and minute of birth—how can we, with finite lives—have been known by God from the beginning? But Julian's words are borne out by the writer to the Ephesians: "Blessed be the God and Father of our Lord Jesus Christ, who has blessed us in Christ with every spiritual blessing in the heavenly places, even as he chose us in him before the foundation of the world, that we should be holy and blameless before him" (Eph. 1:3–4).

Even the psalmist sings of that marvel: "Thou knowest me right well; my frame was not hidden from thee, when I was being made in secret, intricately wrought in the depths of the earth. Thy eyes beheld my unformed substance; in thy book were written, every one of them, the days that were formed for me, when as yet there were none of them" (Ps. 139:14b–16).

God has known us, named us, called us from all time. God did not have to begin loving us, because God's love for us has always been. That is beyond our understanding, but so vital a knowing for us to have: God's love for us knows no beginning, no bounds, and no end.

God of love, you made us your own long before we had breath or form. We praise you for your marvelous work, for we are fearfully and wonderfully made. Grant that we may hear your call, and have confidence in it. Amen

LET YOUR PRAYER BE LARGE

"It is the will of our Lord that our prayer and our trust be large. We must truly know that our Lord is the ground from which prayer sprouts and that it is a gift given out of love, otherwise we waste our time and pain ourselves" (Doyle 1983).

The group gathered in the evening for worship, and the shadows hung dark and rich around the chapel as day's light began to fade. The worshipers began to sing the prayer from the vespers liturgy: "Let my prayer rise before you as incense, the lifting up of my hands as the evening sacrifice. . . ." As they sang, a dancer entered, and carried a bowl containing incense. She raised the bowl high and clouds of incense filled the room. Its pungent smell seemed to transport the worshipers into another time and space, and the ancient words of the psalm they sang became new. In that room, God was great and large—and the prayers God invited took on the largeness and greatness of the billowing smoke of incense.

33

We belong to a God who invites us to pray constantly, and who invites us to ask for what we need, promising that it shall be given to us. Prayer opens us to hear God's Word. Prayer on behalf of other people not only strengthens them, but also enables us to love them and have compassion for them. Prayer allows our own trust of God to grow. So often we make both God and our requests so small that we do not benefit from the greatness of God's mercy and God's ability to fill our hearts and provide for our need.

God is the very ground out of which our prayers grow. We pray because we know God is the source of all things. We may plant and water, but it is God alone who gives the growth. When we let our prayers and our trust be large, as Julian says, we can only be blessed by God's abundant grace.

Most gracious God, you invite us to trust you for all things and to pray without ceasing. Help us to let our prayers be as large and great as your promises. Let our prayers be sweet upon your ears. Amen

JESUS OUR MOTHER

"The human mother will suckle her child with her own milk, but our beloved Mother, Jesus, feeds us with himself, and with the most tender courtesy, does it by means of the Blessed Sacrament, the precious food of all true life" (Julian 1966).

Perhaps the most celebrated and unusual image from Julian's writing is the portrait she gives of Jesus Christ as our mother. In this and several other passages she focuses on a mother "at work": a mother will feed a child, teach and discipline a child, comfort the child who is sad, and cleanse the one who needs to be washed.

Just as mothers work to feed their children, even producing food from their own bodies, so also Jesus feeds us. Julian speaks of Christ "nursing" us to maturity by feeding us from his own body through the means of the Lord's Supper.

It was at the meal table that Jesus took bread and wine, gave thanks for it, and gave it to each one seated there to eat. He told his disciple friends that this was his body and his blood. It was the great gift of himself to feed us and strengthen us.

In a strange way, Jesus does do the things we have long associated with the tasks of mothering. Julian uses that image to show the trust we might have in Christ, the same trust a child has in its mother.

Julian writes further of this: *"The human mother may put her child tenderly to her breast, but our tender Mother Jesus simply leads us into his blessed breast through his open side, and there gives us a glimpse of the Godhead and heavenly joy—the inner certainty of eternal bliss"* (Julian 1966).

Gracious God, in you we find one more motherly than our own mothers, and more fatherly than our own fathers. We give you praise and hearty thanks that you nourish and sustain us with your own body and blood, strengthening us for all we encounter in this life, and guiding us in ways that are in keeping with your will. Grant that we may receive your gifts with believing hearts. Amen

THE OLD AND THE NEW

"In this life there is within us who are to be saved a surprising mixture of good and bad. We have our risen Lord; we have the wretchedness and mischief done by Adam's fall and death. Kept secure by Christ we are assured, by his touch of grace, of salvation; broken by Adam's fall, and in many ways by our own sins and sorrows, we are so darkened and blinded that we can hardly find any comfort" (Julian 1966).

J ulian touches on a compelling truth in this statement: that even when we are confident that we are a "new creation" in Jesus Christ, we still struggle with the old self in us that persists in raising its head. Luther talked about being a saint and a sinner at the same time: a sinner because the struggle with the old self will not be over until we are joined to Christ, and a saint because God graciously views us through eyes that see us as blameless.

That struggle is age-old and difficult. How many times we make efforts to change and to be more faithful. Yet how easily our efforts meet their end. But we have a word that stands over against all of that: "Therefore, if any one is in Christ, he is a new creation; the old has passed away, behold, the new has come" (2 Cor. 5:17). God is at work in us, from the moment of Baptism on, to fashion us into new people—people who trust God to open the future for us. There may not be much evidence of that new creation. But you and I see only from a human point of view. God's view is far different, and God has promised to persevere in making that new creation.

We have signs of the new creation whenever we are given the grace to think of the neighbor before we consider our own well-being, or whenever people are able to trust one another in relationship and open themselves to truth telling and dream sharing. The signs are there, quiet and subtle, but they are there.

God of all life, through your risen Son Jesus Christ you have made us each a new creation. Give us strength to refuse the schemes of the old self—and when we know we cannot, then assure us of your grace and comfort so we may see that Christ does live within us. Amen

THANKS BE TO GOD!

"With prayer goes gratitude. Thanksgiving is a real, interior knowledge. . . . It brings joy and gratitude within. Sometimes its very abundance gives voice, 'Good Lord, thank you and bless you!' And sometimes when the heart is dry and unfeeling—or it may be because of the enemy's tempting—then reason and grace drive us to cry aloud to our Lord, recalling his blessed passion and great goodness. And the strength of our Lord's word comes to the soul, and fires the heart, and leads it by grace into its real business, enabling it to pray happily and to enjoy our Lord in truth" (Julian 1966).

Anna was a woman whose entire life had been marked by her thanksgiving to God. At age 101, she would speak of her gratitude that she and her sister, Clara, could live just two doors apart in the nursing home. She was grateful that they could be well cared for, and be in good health and of sound mind.

In the spring of her 102nd year, the time finally did come for Anna, who had spoken confidently all along about "going home" to her Lord. At the meal following the funeral, friends—some who had had Anna as a Sunday School teacher more than 50 years ago—gathered around her sister to speak words of thanksgiving about Anna. The words of praise were moving: "You and Anna always made me feel like royalty. . . . You were both women of grace. . . ."

Women of grace—that is precisely right. For the gratitude and graciousness of these two women came from living in God's grace, from living in the Word. It had become that "real, interior, knowledge" of which Julian speaks. It is the one thing that sustains through the spiritually dry seasons of our lives. "Time was," reflected Anna's sister, "I thought I could manage everything on my own. Finally, late in life, I learned that there was someone else who could manage it all better than I. Now I ask for help. And it is there."

Anna and Clara knew, as did Julian, that "the Word fires the heart," leading us deeper into the abundant promises of God's grace, and giving us hearts made for thanksgiving.

Gracious and loving God, thank you for the countless gifts of each new day. Make us good stewards of your gifts. Amen

THOMAS À KEMPIS

Robert Stackel

IT IS CLAIMED THAT THE DEVOTIONAL BOOK *The Imitation of Christ* by Thomas à Kempis (ca. 1380–1471), has been, next to the Bible, the most popular spiritual reading in the whole world for over five hundred years. It has been translated into more than fifty languages and has been beloved by Christians of all different types.

It was written originally in Latin and hand copied for decades before the invention of the printing press. Although there are still more than seven hundred manuscript copies of his book in existence, most publications today are translations of a 1441 manuscript written by Thomas's own hand, which is the definitive text. The humility of Thomas kept him from signing his name to his writings.

Thomas was born in the little Rhineland town of Kempen near Düsseldorf (hence, Thomas from Kempen) in the year 1379 or 1380, the son of an artisan. When Thomas was 20, he felt the call to the religious life and applied for entrance into a new religious community called Mount St. Agnes near Zwolle. Eventually he took his vows and was ordained a priest in 1413. He fulfilled the usual round of monastic duties: reading and studying, copying and writing books, and training of novices. As a priest dealing with people in the confessional and in counseling, he learned the depths of human sorrow and the heights of spiritual joy. He steeped himself in the knowledge of the Scriptures and in time became a master of novices, training them in the religious life. He also wrote about how the spiritual insights he had discovered related to the experiences of life. The *Imitation* grew out of his instructions to novices. We don't know much about the rest of Thomas's life. For more than seventy years he lived at Mount St. Agnes, dying there on May 1, 1471, after Compline, when he was 91.

The vast popularity of the *Imitation* is due to its simplicity, its deep spirituality, and its keen interpretation of Scripture. Its style resembles that of Scripture itself, and often Scripture is quoted in it. Its timeless truth speaks to all humanity. The book was written at a time when a new Europe was emerging and the laity were acquiring a more prominent role in the life of the church. The established institutions of the church could not handle the new situation very well, so Thomas wrote to penetrate the new order with a profound spiritual piety. His piety has a rich contribution to make to Christians of all ages, all cultures, and all places.

THE TEST OF TRUTH

"If you would understand Christ's words fully and taste them truly, you must strive to form your whole life after his pattern."

I f anyone wants to understand more perfectly the teachings of another person, one must live those teachings and so test them. To understand better the convictions of an environmentalist, one must practice living in a way so as to do the least harm to the environment and discover what kind of a feeling this brings. To understand better the principles of a vegetarian, one must practice eating no meat for a time to discover what impression that makes.

Jesus welcomes our putting his teachings to the test by practicing them in daily life. If they work out in actual life, then they must be true. Take forgiveness, for example, which Jesus taught and lived. When we forgive someone an intentional wrong, do we feel good about it in our hearts? Is the other person blessed by it? Is the world a better place because of it? Or think of self-denial for the sake of others. When we deny ourselves some pleasure in order to help someone in trouble, do we have a good feeling about it inwardly? Is the other person happier? Does this please God?

Jesus once said, "If any man's will is to do [God's] will, he shall know whether the teaching is from God or whether I am speaking on my own authority" (John 7:17). Notice that the verb is *do,* not just talk about it. To do it is to put it into practice in daily life. God wants us to test his teachings in the crucible of actual life. He, the creator of all life, knows that his teachings, when practiced, enrich life as nothing else can.

Lord Jesus Christ, you came that we might have life. Give us the will to live the truths you taught, and in living them to discover new depths of joy and peace and a new closeness to you, our way to God the Father. In your name we pray. Amen

USES OF ADVERSITY

"It is good for us at times to have troubles and adversities; for often they make a man enter into himself, so that he may know that he is in exile, and may not place his hopes in anything of this world."

Thomas had a positive approach to setbacks. Instead of whining about them, he advised discovering their use. Every trouble has some use for the person who is willing to seek diligently enough with the Holy Spirit's help to find it.

A father took his twelve-year-old son out for his first rifle practice. The son raised the gun and fired as his father had instructed him. The blast of the gun nearly scared the boy out of his wits, and the powerful recoil of the rifle threw him backward into his father's arms; his father, anticipating this very thing, had taken a position behind his son to catch him. It was with a new appreciation of his father that the boy pulled himself together again. Life is like that. The shock of some experience unnerves us, and the recoil throws us backwards. That is, it seems as though it is backwards, but then we find ourself in our Father's arms, who was waiting to catch us and support us.

Thomas described a person in this world as being "in exile." He meant that this world is not our home. We are only pilgrims traveling through this life. Our true home is in heaven. Therefore, we should not look primarily to anything in this world to restore us when we fall into trouble, but to God, our loving heavenly Father. Thomas counseled: "Therefore ought a man to establish himself so firmly in God that he has no need to seek many human consolations."

St. Paul knew the meaning of trouble. He spoke of his "thorn in the flesh" and prayed to God agonizingly and repeatedly for its removal. But God didn't take away his thorn. Instead, God gave Paul something far better, namely, this assurance: "My grace is sufficient for you, for my power is made perfect in weakness" (2 Cor. 12:9).

O Holy Spirit, turn for us life's disappointing setbacks into experiences that move us forward spiritually, through Christ, whose cross was turned into a crown. Amen

ON LOOKING AHEAD

"A very little while and all will be over with you here. Ask yourself are you ready for the next life? . . . O the dullness and the hardness of the human heart, that dwells only upon things present, instead of providing rather for those which are to come! You should so order yourself in every deed and thought as though you were to die this day. . . . If you are not prepared today, how will you be tomorrow? Tomorrow is an uncertain day; and how do you know if you shall have tomorrow?"

The uncertainty of the length of a human life weighed heavily on Thomas, as it should upon us all. "When it is morning, think that you will not live till evening," he wrote. "And when evening comes, venture not to promise yourself the next morning. Therefore be always ready; and so live that death may never find you unprepared." He also wrote, "Of what use is it to live long, when we amend ourselves so little?" And then, "How happy and how prudent is he who strives to be in life what he would fain be found in death!" But also, "The time will come when you will desire one day or even one hour for amendment; and I know not if you will obtain it."

His words in *The Imitation of Christ* are like an echo of Christ's words in Mark about the end. "Take heed, watch," Jesus taught, "for you do not know when the time will come." Then Jesus told his disciples the parable about the master of a household going away on a long trip, putting the servants in charge, not knowing when he would return.

Thomas continued: "Therefore, study so to live now that in the hour of death you may be able to rejoice rather than be afraid. Learn now to die to the world, that then you may begin to live with Christ." He concluded, "Think of nothing but your salvation; care only for the things of God."

Lord Jesus Christ, we long for your return to earth in glory. Keep us watchful, spiritually prepared, and always amending our life. Take us in your mercy to our home with the Father. We pray in your dear name. Amen

SOLITUDE AND SILENCE

"Seek a convenient time to retire into yourself; and think often on the benefits of God."

A modern problem is that there is no "convenient time" to draw apart for a silent time with God in our overscheduled days. Besides, we are afraid of silence. The television or radio must always be on. We are more afraid of silence than we are of noise.

As if speaking to our day, Thomas wrote, "He, therefore, who aims at inward and spiritual things, must with Jesus turn aside from the crowd." This is almost a mirror image of what Jesus told the disciples in Mark: "Come away by yourselves to a lonely place, and rest awhile" (Mark 6:31). Jesus' next sentence sounds like the twenty-first century: "For many were coming and going, and they had no leisure even to eat."

Thomas insisted, "In silence and in quiet the devout soul makes progress, and learns the hidden things of Scripture." Then he added, "For who so withdraws himself from his acquaintances and friends, to him will God draw near with his holy angels." And also, "If you would feel compunction to your very heart, retire to your room and shut out the noise of the world." This sounds like Jesus speaking in Matthew: "When you pray, go into your room and shut the door and pray to your Father who sees in secret" (Matt. 6:6).

When the prophet Elijah stood on the mountain, God wanted to speak to him (1 Kings 19:11–13). A mighty wind came up, but God was not in the wind. Then came an earthquake, but God was not in the earthquake. Then followed a raging fire, but God was not in the fire. Finally there was "a still small voice." That was God speaking. How can we hear God's soft whisper of a voice unless we withdraw from the noise of the world and listen to him in the silence of his presence with an open Bible?

Heavenly Father, as your Son calmed the storm on Galilee, calm the storm of noise around us. In the silence of your presence speak so that we may hear even your soft whisper of a voice. In Jesus' name we pray. Amen

CULTIVATE THE INNER LIFE

"Many are [Christ's] visits to the man of inward life. With such a one He holds delightful converse, granting him sweet comfort, much peace, and an intimacy astonishing beyond measure."

In his training of candidates for holy orders in the church, Thomas stressed the importance of the inner life. It is just as important for every Christian today. Cultivating the inner life with Christ is not so much a duty as it is a privilege which brings us divine comfort, peace, and union with Christ.

We often fall into the trap of judging someone by outward appearances. Even the venerable prophet, Samuel, once fell into that trap. When God wanted to pick a new king for Israel, he had the sons of Jesse pass before Samuel one by one (1 Sam. 16:6–13). When Eliab stepped forward Samuel thought he was the one. Eliab must have been handsome, strong, and of regal bearing—a Mr. America type. But God said to Samuel, "Do not look on his appearance or on the height of his stature, because I have rejected him; for the Lord sees not as man sees; man looks on the outward appearance, but the Lord looks on the heart." On that basis David was chosen king.

God comes to us in Christ through the Holy Scriptures by the power of the Holy Spirit. The more we hear, read, study, and meditate upon God's word with believing hearts, the deeper and richer our inner life will become and the closer we will be to our Savior God.

Thomas saw the heart and center of God's Word as the suffering death of God's Son for the sin of the world, followed by his victorious resurrection. So he wrote, "If you fly devoutly to the wounds of Jesus and the precious marks of His passion, you shall feel greatly strengthened in tribulation." And again, "Rest in the passion of Christ, and love to dwell within His sacred wounds."

O God, by the power of your Holy Spirit come ever more deeply into our hearts through your holy Word and cause our slain but risen Redeemer to sit on the throne of our lives, for his sake. Amen

43

THE BLESSINGS OF GOD'S LOVE

"Ah, Lord God, my holy Lover! when Thou comest into my heart, all that is within me shall exult with joy. Thou art my glory and the exultation of my heart. Thou art my hope and my refuge in the day of my tribulation."

Thomas treasured with all his heart God's love for him. He called God "my holy Lover." God's love was the pride and joy of his life. He wrote: "The noble love of Jesus impels a man to do great things, and ever excites him to desire that which is more perfect." How similar this sounds to St. Paul's "the love of Christ controls us" (2 Cor. 5:14)!

There is nothing in all creation like the love of God in Christ. He created us in his image and gave us immense resources to resist temptation. When we sin, in spite of it all, he grieves with a broken heart and keeps tugging at our souls through his Holy Spirit to return to him. When we return in repentant trust, he always welcomes us back with open arms for Jesus' sake.

What could impel a gifted person like Thomas à Kempis to a monastery to train beginners in the monastic order except the love of God in Christ? What could transform you into a humble, faithful, grateful disciple of the Savior except the love of God through his slain but risen Son? There is more encouragement, comfort, motivation, and empowerment in God's grace than we have ever begun to harness.

"Nothing is sweeter than love," Thomas wrote. "Nothing stronger, nothing higher, nothing wider, nothing more pleasant, nothing fuller or better in heaven or in earth; for love is born of God, and cannot rest but in God, above all created things." He also wrote, "A lover must willingly embrace all that is hard and bitter for the sake of his Beloved, and never suffer himself to be turned away from Him by any obstacle whatsoever." Can you imitate Christ in that way today?

Let your saving love, O God, so bathe our souls today that we may love others around us with an authentic imitation of Jesus' self-denying love. Amen

CAST ALL CARE ON GOD

*"My son, let Me do with you what I will; I know what is expedient for you.
. . . Lord, what Thou sayest is true. Greater is Thy care for me than all the
care I can take of myself. . . . For it cannot but be good, whatever Thou shalt
do with me."*

During World War II, an English scrubwoman was asked how
she slept so soundly through those terrible nights when
German planes were bombing the city. Her explanation
was: "The good Lord promised that he would watch over us, and I
trust him. There's no sense in two of us staying awake all night."

Thomas similarly trusted in God's gracious providence. He
wrote: "You must be as ready to suffer as to rejoice; you must be as
glad to be poor and needy as to be full and rich." He also said,
"Provided that Thou dost not cast me off for ever, nor blot me out
of the book of life, no matter what tribulation befalls me, it shall
not hurt me."

Peter put it in plain words in his first New Testament letter:
"Cast all your anxieties on him, for he cares about you" (1 Peter 5:7).
Paul wrote the same thing to the Philippians in different words:
"Have no anxiety about anything, but . . . by prayer and thanksgiving
let your requests be made known to God" (Phil. 4:6). Both of them
remembered Jesus' teachings: "Do not be anxious about tomorrow,
for tomorrow will be anxious for itself" (Matt. 6:34).

Anxiety and worry are pollution to the Christian. The London
plane tree is beautifully adapted to living in pollution-laden city air.
Its smooth leaves make it easy for the rain to wash off the city's
grime. It sheds its bark periodically in large, flaky pieces, thus getting rid of impurities embedded in its bark. So, too, Christians can
let God's reign wash off the grime of anxiety and help shed worry
and care like a plane tree sheds its bark. Anxiety cannot stick, for
God has said, "I will never fail you nor forsake you."

*O thou who sees the sparrows fall and clothes the lily, teach us to trust in
your loving providence at all times. Our anxieties do not honor you; we confess with shame our lack of faith. Keep us ever in the hollow of your hand,
through Jesus Christ our Lord. Amen*

GOD IS SWEET

"Thou art my God and my all! What would I have more, and what greater happiness can I desire? . . . For when Thou art present, all things yield delight; but when Thou art absent, all things grow loathsome. Thou makest a tranquil heart, and great peace, and festal joy."

Jaroslav Pelikan described Martin Luther as a "Christ-intoxicated" person. Luther was filled to overflowing with the grace of God in Jesus Christ. Dwight L. Moody once said that he wanted to be so full of the love of God that all the world would see what God could do with a totally dedicated person.

Thomas had trouble putting down the human passions within him to make more room for God in his heart. "As yet," he confessed, "alas, the old man is living in me; he is not wholly crucified; he is not perfectly dead. He still lusts strongly against the spirit and wages war within me." St. Paul knew well that war within. "For I do not do the good I want," he confessed to the church in Rome, "but the evil I do not want is what I do" (Rom. 7:19). Both men wanted most of all to let God fill their lives totally. Thomas wrote, "O when will that blessed and desirable hour come that Thou mayest fill me with Thy presence, and become to me all in all?"

Thomas declared that God is "sweet." We ourselves may not often call God sweet, but the gifts he brings with his presence in our hearts surely are sweet. Thomas says they include "a tranquil heart, and great peace, and festal joy." The psalmist boasted that the Word of God is "sweeter also than honey" (Ps. 19:10). Jackie Gleason, the comedian, had a frequently repeated saying, "How sweet it is!" The Christian believer, rejoicing over Christ within, filled with the presence of God, and possessing the gifts of the Spirit, can exclaim with bubbling enthusiasm, "How sweet it is!"

O God, whose sweetest gift is always yourself, flood our hearts with your gracious presence, filling every hidden crevice until deep within we may wear an unfading smile freshened by tranquility, peace, and joy, through Jesus Christ we pray. Amen

LIFE AT THE CROSS-ROAD

"My son, in proportion as you can go out of yourself, so will you be able to enter into Me. Just as the desiring no outward thing brings inward peace, so does the forsaking of yourself inwardly bring union with God."

homas reminded his readers that Jesus told his followers that whoever keeps his commands is the one who loves him. Those who hold to Jesus' teaching are really his disciples. They will know the truth and the truth will make them free. To those who overcome, Jesus will give the right to sit with him on his throne.

In his *Imitation of Christ,* Thomas amplified those words with "I will have you learn the perfect renunciation of yourself to My will, without contradiction or complaint." Much depends on *how* a person bears the cross. Resentfully? Complainingly? With self-pity? Or cheerfully, patiently and without complaint? Scripture says, "Jesus . . . for the joy that was set before him endured the cross, despising the shame" (Heb. 12:2). He rejoiced in heart, though tortured in body, that he was emancipating all believers from sin and that he was fulfilling his Father's will. A cross isn't as heavy when those twin joys—ministering to others and doing God's will—are in the heart.

Jesus taught, "If any man would come after me, let him deny himself and take up his cross and follow me" (Matt. 16:24). Thomas replied, "Let us follow Him like [mature adults]; let no one fear any terrors; . . . and let us not stain our glory by flying from the cross." Thomas has a beautiful passage: "'Follow Me,' Jesus says: 'I am the way, the truth, and the life.' Without the way there is no going; without the truth there is no knowing; without the life there is no living. I am the way which you should follow, the truth which you should believe, the life which you should hope for. I am the way inviolable, the truth infallible, the life everlasting."

Lord Jesus, grant that we may follow you in bearing the world's contempt. Help us to be instructed by your life, for it is the source of salvation and true holiness. Amen

FAITH HAS CLENCHED FINGERS

"I had rather be poor for Thy sake than rich without Thee. I had rather be a pilgrim upon earth with Thee than possess heaven without Thee. Where Thou art, there is heaven; and where Thou art not, there are death and hell."

I n addition to the above words, Thomas wrote, "Thou art my hope, my confidence, my comforter, and in all things most faithful." It is obvious that Thomas clung to God for dear life.

In Portland, Maine, a commuter airline pilot named Henry Dempsey was aloft in flight when he heard a rattle in the back of the plane and went to investigate, leaving the copilot at the controls. As Dempsey leaned against the rear door, the plane struck some air turbulence. The door suddenly flew open, sucking him out at 4,000 feet. He had the presence of mind in a split second to grab the railings of the stairway door, and there he hung upside down as the plane cruised along at 190 miles per hour. When it made an emergency landing, Dempsey's face was one foot above the concrete runway. An airline spokesman said that the pilot's hands were clenched so tightly around the railings of the stairway door that they literally had to be pried off. Said the pilot the next day, "I was thrilled to see the sunrise."

Suppose that we clenched the promises of God so tightly that our fingers of faith would literally have to be pried off if ever we were to be separated. Here's a promise of God in Hebrews: "I will never fail you nor forsake you" (Heb. 13:5). If life turned you upside down in some sudden disturbance, faith could hold onto that promise with clenched fingers and bring you down safely. Nothing can pry loose the curl of our fingers around Christ. Holding onto him, we shall always see another sunrise.

Thomas prayed: *Protect and preserve the soul of Thy poor servant amidst the many perils of this corruptible life, and by Thy accompanying grace direct him along the path of peace to his native country of everlasting light. Amen*

MARTIN LUTHER

Jane Strohl

MARTIN LUTHER (1483–1546) WAS BORN IN SAXONY, AND HIS parents saw to it that he received a good education. He was embarking on studies for a career in law when an extraordinary experience elicited from him a vow that changed the course of his life forever. Caught in a violent thunderstorm, Luther prayed to St. Anne for assistance, promising that if he were delivered from danger, he would become a monk. He was and he did, astonishing and dismaying his friends and family.

Luther entered the Augustinian cloister in Erfurt. His superior, Johann von Staupitz, then determined that the gifted young man should return to school to take his doctor's degree and teach. Luther became a professor of Scripture at the University of Wittenburg. Luther wrote near the end of his life that a new understanding of Romans 1:17 led him to a resolution of the conflict tormenting his conscience: "Then, finally, God had mercy on me, and I began to understand that the righteousness of God is that gift of God by which a righteous man lives, namely, faith, and that his sentence—the righteousness of God is revealed in the Gospel—is passive, indicating that the merciful God justifies us by faith. . . . Now I felt as though I had been reborn altogether and had entered Paradise" (Luther 1951).

One might describe Luther's career as a lifelong pastoral malpractice suit against the Roman Catholic hierarchy of his day, whose doctrine of grace, in his opinion, deprived believers of true consolation and robbed Christ of His rightful honor as Savior. Yet the years brought conflicts with other groups in which he felt called to champion the cause of the gospel as he understood it. Luther's theology was polemical, his style often inflammatory. The heirs to his legacy often feel compelled to apologize for him. Indeed, a fair and critical evaluation of his work requires that one acknowledge inconsistencies, errors of judgment, and attitudes that are disturbing. But the same fair and critical eye cannot help but recognize the force of his confession and the keen insight of his spiritual guidance. Luther challenges each generation to measure its understanding of the gospel against the message he found to be the heart of Scripture: "For the person is justified and saved, not by works or laws, but by the Word of God, that is, by the promise of his grace, and by faith, that the glory may remain God's, who saved us not by works of righteousness which we have done, but by virtue of his mercy by the word of his grace when we believed" (Luther 1957).

ST. CHRISTOPHER'S BURDEN

"When one receives the faith, one does not allow oneself to imagine that there will be difficulty in this. . . . It appears to one as a tiny child, pretty and well formed and easy to carry. For the Gospel shows itself at first as a fine, pleasing, friendly, and childlike doctrine, as we then saw at the start, when everyone seized upon it and wanted to be evangelical. There was such longing and thirst for the Gospel that no oven's heat could match that of the people then. But what happened? The same situation occurred as befell Christopher, who did not learn how heavy the little child was until he had entered the deepest water" (Luther 1906).

L uther preached these words in a sermon delivered to the Elector of Saxony and his party just before their departure for the Diet of Augsburg in 1530. This gathering was summoned by the Emperor Charles V, so that those who had embraced Luther's teaching would have to give account of the faith that was in them. If the Emperor was unconvinced by their testimony, he could use military force against his Protestant subjects.

In this sermon Luther sought to prepare his friends and their prince for the trial that lay ahead. He tells them of St. Christopher, who, according to legend, bore the little Christ with joy and ease at first. Yet as he forded deep water, Christopher felt himself dragged down by the child. The gospel, says Luther, is lovely and irresistible to the believer at the start. But to hold fast to the Word is not easy. To confess Christ before those who challenge our conviction, to trust God in the midst of suffering, to press on with our burden of faithfulness—these, too, are part of what it means to be a Christian. Luther acknowledges to his hearers that they enter the waters at great risk, but he also reminds them of the promises of God, extending like strong, stout branches from the opposite shore to support them in the tide.

Lord Jesus Christ, never remove the weight of your presence from our lives. Let us lean upon you in our times of weakness and trial, and bring us safely through them. Amen

DOUBT

"But when one's head begins to swim, when one is obliged to taste the experience and bring it into one's life, then understanding comes very dear. It is well nigh unbearable that we should lose the Christ in us, the one we believe to be God's Son who died and rose for us, and that he should die to us, as happened to the apostles throughout the three days. Then there takes place a miserable crucifixion and dying, when Christ dies in me and I also to him. As he says here: 'You will not see me, for I am going from you,' that is, I am dying; so you will also die because you see me not and thus will I be dead to you and you to me. Only then do we really know extraordinary, deep, grievous sorrow"(Luther 1913).

Luther talked about God as being both hidden and revealed. As the Christmas communion liturgy proclaims, the God whom we see revealed in Jesus Christ comes to us so that we may come to worship, love, and trust the God whom we do not see.

In the witness of Scripture, the history of humankind, and the sorrows of our own private stories we see reasons not only to be mystified by God's ways but distrustful, even terrified of God. The Gospel is compelling evidence to the contrary, says Luther, but even after Christ's entrance into our lives, we do not feel unfailingly secure. The snares of doubt can still encompass us. We shall know the kind of emptiness and despair which afflicted the disciples after the Lord's crucifixion. Yet foretelling his absence, Christ also promised his return: "A little while, and you will see me no more; again a little while, and you will see me." So we must hold onto the promise in our time of loss and lean upon the faith of our friends to sustain us.

Lord Jesus, it is not easy for us to bear the times when we feel you absent from our lives. Yet to know uncertainty and grief, to fear abandonment by the One we have trusted and loved is to follow in the way of the disciples and indeed of you yourself. Grant that we, too, may be restored to joy and raised to new life. Amen

THE WORD

"Therefore our life is simply contained in the bare Word; for we have Christ, we have eternal life, eternal righteousness, help and comfort, but where is it? We don't see it. We neither possess it in coffers nor hold it in our hands, but only in the bare Word. Thus has God clothed his object in nothingness" (Luther 1906).

Our desire to retain control over things great and small is the root of what Luther identified as our besetting sin, works-righteousness. It is so easy, he said, to slip from receiving a gift to earning a reward. We want to build salvation out of our own works and initiate, determine, and control. We want to give ourselves identity and to create meaning for our lives by our efforts and achievement. Yet God will not have it so. It is not that God denies us our own active role in the world. We must never underestimate the importance of our works, but we must avoid false understandings of them as well. It is blessed to give to our neighbors through an active, creative life, but when it comes to God, it is more blessed to receive—that "bare Word" of promise, which we can neither see nor seize and hold in our own safekeeping.

53

Our salvation is, as Luther puts it, clothed in nothingness. It is God's gift, borne by the seemingly insubstantial sound of a voice. We never know when we shall hear God's word in, with, and under the many human words addressed to us. We never know when that word will echo so resoundingly in our hearts, stilling pain, unmasking sin, and sowing hope, that our lives take an unexpected direction. The hardest fight is to accept that we cannot control this word. We must let God be God.

Gracious Lord, keep us steadfast in your Word. Give us ears to hear, wisdom to understand and courage to respond. Teach us confidently to receive what you would give and to surrender to you the control we covet for ourselves. Amen

RIGHTEOUSNESS

"You see that the First Commandment, which says, 'You shall worship one God,' is fulfilled by faith alone. Though you were nothing but good works from the soles of your feet to the crown of your head, you would still not be righteous or worship God or fulfill the First Commandment, since God cannot be worshiped unless you ascribe to him the glory of truthfulness and all goodness which is due him. This cannot be done by works but only by the faith of the heart"(Luther 1957).

Once again Luther is telling us that nothing should come between us and God, not even our good works. For though it seems that we might rightfully be proud of these, Luther insists that they cannot make us righteous. Indeed, if we depend upon them to give us claims before God, then our very "right doing" leads us into the worst of sins, the breaking of the first and chief commandment. To look to our own actions for our salvation is to have another god in place of the One who should command our hearts and receive our worship.

54

In our efforts to please God by keeping the commandments, we can all too easily defy God's will. We withhold something of ourselves. Surreptitiously we keep some element of control, hoping to respond to God's challenge with a righteousness of our own. We are loath to appear empty-handed, to acknowledge and offer to God our vulnerability. But this is what God asks of us. It is a fearsome demand for intimacy and honesty and trust. When we fall back on our works, we beg God's question. To lay aside all righteousness of our own and to rest solely on the promise that God wills to be our Lord in life and death, this is the worship God desires from us. This is the true source of all righteousness.

Gracious God, we give you thanks for being our God. Create faith in us to respond to your faithfulness. Let our good works abound but not come between us and your grace. In Christ's name we pray. Amen

Psalm 23

"The Lord certainly makes of me a strange warrior and arms me against my enemies in an unusual manner. I thought he should clothe me with a suit of armor, set a helmet on my head, put a sword in my hand and warn me to be cautious and on the lookout constantly, lest my enemies overtake me. So he sits me at a table and prepares for me a feast, anoints my head with precious balsam or crowns me with a garland, as if I should go rejoicing and dancing and not do battle with my enemies. So the prepared table is my armor, the precious balsam my helmet, the proffered overflowing cup my sword with which I overcome all my enemies. Is this not a singular armor and an even more singular victory?"(Luther 1914).

Luther writes of the trials and hardships that attend faith. He lived in difficult times, when the threat of persecution was often real. But the dangers were not only external. As we have seen, Luther knew the doubt and fear that could beset the conscience from within and cause the believer great anguish. The confession of the gospel of Jesus Christ often weighed heavily upon him, like the burden of the Christ child dragging St. Christopher down. Yet the gospel, like the lovely child, was always a source of wonder and delight.

This commentary on Psalm 23 shows that, along with temptation and opposition, Luther also knew ecstasy in his service of the Lord. He never ceased to marvel at the power of God. This soldier in defense of the gospel might well expect grim duty. Yet the Lord prepares him for his place on the front lines not with harsh discipline but with feasting and celebration.

Luther reflects on the momentous events of which he has been a part and sees God carrying out great things through commonplace persons and actions. Looking at our own lives, we, too, can find cause for wonder and rejoicing at God's guiding hand.

Gracious God, refresh us at your table so that even in hardship we may go our way rejoicing in you. In Christ's name we pray. Amen

LIFE IN CHRIST

"Thus, as long as the danger and uncertainty of death are present, so long am I to believe that Christ is my life, that is, the whole time that I am here on earth. Let no one evaluate this proclamation according to the hour, season or year—it never becomes null and void so that you dare say, 'Christ will be my life when the time comes for me to die, meanwhile I shall live as I please.' But you should know that the time has already come for you to make that crossing. You have already stepped into the sea with the children of Israel, and you must press on until you come to the shore, lest the enemy seize you under way" (Luther 1911).

Some people come to know Christ in one dramatic encounter. Their hearts are pierced, their eyes opened, and never again can they return to their old ways and beliefs. One thinks here of St. Paul and his experience on the road to Damascus. For others of us, the process of conversion is far more gradual, at times imperceptible. God nudges, fascinates, and frustrates us in numerous incidents, making us mindful of our lives in new ways. The critical point may well come with some misfortune—the estrangement of a loved one, the failure of a career, the onset of illness. We are made keenly aware of our vulnerability and our powerlessness to set things right in our world. We learn that sometimes we must endure conditions and situations that are painful and unjust. We learn what it is to suffer and thus taste our mortality. Then we are drawn to a savior like Christ, one who loves in the midst of cruelty and brings life from death.

Yet Luther reminds us that Christ is our Lord every day. Life for Luther is a pilgrimage with God. It is not only at its unmistakably sharp edges, in times of sorrow and disappointment and on the verge of death, that one must dare to live in Christ. Every hour, every season, every year is crucial: "You have already stepped into the sea with the children of Israel and you must press on . . ."

Lord Jesus, be our life now and at the hour of our death. Every day is a crossing; in your mercy, guide and keep us safe. Amen

THE RESURRECTION

"But Christ, on the other hand, is a lord and prince of life beyond all the power of the devil. Therefore he leads his own and brings them with him to heaven, because they are in him, and they live and die and lie in his bosom and arms, not in the grave or in the power of the devil, except in the old being. Just as Christ also, though he lay in the grave, yet in a moment he was both dead and alive and rose again like a lightening flash from heaven. So he will raise us too in an instant, in the twinkling of an eye, out of the grave, the dust, the water, and we shall stand in full view, utterly pure and clean as the bright sun. This is what St. Paul certainly wants us to conclude and believe (though it is incredible and ridiculous to reason) as a sure consequence of the fact that Christ died and rose again"(Luther 1959).

S ome people feel that Christian teaching about the hereafter has led to the neglect of this world and the endurance of wrong in the name of a better life to come. We need not turn away from this world and fix our hopes on a new heaven and earth, they say. Rather, we can draw on the grace and guidance that are ours in Christ Jesus to transform the creation and realize human life in this world according to the new Adam. These are important understandings of the power and meaning of Christ's resurrection. Yet they often relegate the afterlife to an afterthought in Christian theology or dismiss it from consideration altogether.

We are drawn to contemplate the lordship of Christ in the light of eternity, to ponder what it means to confess Him as the prince of life. When we bury our dead, there is more at stake than the meaning of the resurrection for life in this world. Luther reminds those who gather to mourn that while they have good cause for sorrow, they have even greater cause for hope. Christ came into the world to claim us as the children of the living God; the claim holds good whether we walk the earth or lie in the grave. Where do we go when we die? We go to the One who is already with us.

Jesus our Savior, grant that by the power of your resurrection we may live and die boldly under your lordship. Amen

THE LORD'S SUPPER

"The need (which drives us to [the Lord's Supper]) is that sin, devil, and death are always present. The benefit is that we receive forgiveness of sins and the Holy Spirit. Here, not poison, but a remedy and salvation is given, in so far as you acknowledge that you need it. Don't say: I am not fit today, I will wait a while. This is a trick of the devil. What will you do if you are not fit when death comes? Who will make you fit then? Say rather: Neither preacher, prince, pope, nor emperor compels me, but my great need and, beyond this, the benefit" (Luther 1959).

L uther worried about the infrequency with which many Christians came to the Lord's table in his day. Some felt no need, and Luther sternly cautioned them that such an attitude was a clear indication of peril. When one's spirit is not troubled by the consciousness of sin and experiences no hunger for mercy and reconciliation, then one is desperately in need of grace. At such times we are the least competent judges of our condition and must be "sinners by faith," that is, we must take God's word as to the depth of our brokenness and alienation.

Others hesitated to receive the sacrament because of a painful sense of their unworthiness. One does not determine when to be baptized according to the strength of one's faith, nor does one wait until one feels deserving to come to the Lord's table. The sacrament does not demand righteousness, it imparts it; it creates the faith it requires. Humility in this instance may not serve us well. Our conviction of unworthiness may foster the drive to make ourselves "fit" and thus to assume some responsibility for our own salvation. Time and again Luther reminds us that God doesn't give grace on such terms. When you look at yourself and see your great need, let it turn you to Christ, not in on yourself. Forgiveness of sin and the gifts of the Spirit wait for you there, the very things you need to be fit for service and salvation.

Gracious Lord Jesus, teach us to know our great need, bring us to your table, and fill us with your grace. Amen

SIN AND SANCTIFICATION

"Contrariwise, we teach and comfort the afflicted sinner after this manner: Brother, it is not possible for thee to become so righteous in this life, that thou shouldest feel no sin at all, that thy body should be clear like the sun, without spot or blemish; but thou hast as yet wrinkles and spots, and yet art thou holy notwithstanding. But thou wilt say: How can I be holy, when I have and feel sin in me? I answer: In that thou dost feel and acknowledge thy sin, it is a good token; give thanks unto God and despair not. It is one step of health, when the sick man doth acknowledge and confess his infirmity. But how shall I be delivered from sin? Run to Christ the physician, which healeth them that are broken in heart, and saveth sinners" (Luther 1953, 1956).

Luther expected believers to struggle with their discipleship, to labor daily to conform their lives to Christ, and to make real progress. When you are giving thanks, reflect over your own life and recognize the number of harmful attitudes and actions you have rejected, the set of new habits you have cultivated because of Christ's challenging presence in your life. Even as we see how much remains to be changed, we can look forward with hope because of the transformations that have already occurred under Christ's guidance and care.

Yet Luther knew better than to let people dwell on their sanctification, for it can also be disheartening. The life of discipleship is not one of steady advance. Too often our old faults reassert themselves. Time and time again God's Word sounds out in judgment upon us. It pierces the heart, and we feel shame. How can I be holy, the frustrated believer cries, when I cannot escape sin? I thought I was moving toward heaven, but here I am in hell again. Ah yes, says Luther, but this hell is the forecourt of paradise. "It is one step of health, when the sick man doth acknowledge and confess his infirmity." And the next step takes one to Christ and his healing righteousness.

Lord Jesus, be near us when sin rages so that we may turn to you to find hope, forgiveness, and the power to amend our lives. Amen

UNBELIEVERS

"For everything happens according to Christ's counsel, will, and ordaining. Without and beyond him nothing occurs. If something good transpires through pious princes and rulers, Christ sets it in motion and advances it. Should something evil take place through wicked rulers and tyrants, he decrees it. How it comes about, however, that he holds everything in his hands, rules, creates, effects, propels, and preserves, and yet not all people are godly, this belongs to the invisible rule of the invisible God, which it is not fitting for us to investigate"(Luther 1911).

Because our relationship to Christ is so fundamental to our existence, we want other people to experience Christ's presence. Indeed we are charged to bear witness to him so that others might hear the Word and be transformed by its power. Yet the mystery remains—why are not all people godly?

Some of the blame may well lie with us. Perhaps our efforts at evangelizing have been clumsy, our message unclear, and our manner insensitive. Certainly we need to attend to such matters. Yet all our art and wisdom cannot guarantee the success of our mission. The source of the Word's power is God. We may sound it in the ears of our neighbors, but only God can seal it in their hearts. Even when we think we are coming to Christ and making a decision for him on our own, it is God bringing us and creating in us new powers of love and faithfulness. So what are we to say of those who seem to remain unmoved? Have they rejected God or has God rejected them?

It may not be a very satisfying answer that Luther gives, but it is an honest one. When we recognize that "everything happens according to Christ's counsel," we must acknowledge that this counsel often mystifies, even terrifies us. Yet it assures us that Christ has the power to do what he has promised, that is, to save. When faced with the mystery of God's ways, we can only commend all of humankind to the certainty of God's grace.

Gracious Lord, claim for your own all whom you have created. This we ask in Christ's name. Amen

BROTHER LAWRENCE

Vernon Schreiber

HE WAS A KITCHEN COOK WHO BECAME THE SPIRITUAL DIRECTOR of his superiors. He objected to being published and left behind letters more cherished with each passing century. He scrupulously fulfilled his vows of obedience and became the freest of spirits. He described himself as a "clumsy lummox" who broke everything but sculpted his life into a thing of beauty. He spent his last forty years inside monastery walls and became a pioneer carving out a new highway to God. He offered himself to the Lord in a spirit of subjection and self-denial and was surprised to find a life of joy. Expecting nothing, he found so much that he often said to God, "You have outwitted me." His name was Brother Lawrence (1608 or 1611–1691).

Born Nicholas Herman, in Lorraine, France, he was, according to his own report, converted at the age of 18. Gazing at a tree in early spring, knowing that soon it would burst forth into buds and then leaves, he became overwhelmed with the awareness of the providence and power of God and by God's grace, was filled with a love for God that never diminished.

As a young man he served as a soldier in what came to be known as the Thirty Years War. He was wounded and discharged. He then decided to give his life wholly to Christ, first choosing the life of a hermit. He soon saw that this was not for him and applied for admission to a Carmelite monastery. He was admitted and became a full member of his order in 1642.

He did not immediately burst forth into lofty thoughts about God. He learned what all must learn: "One does not become holy all at once." But then something happened and he began to experience "a profound interior peace." He had learned to practice the presence of God. When he died his painful death, it was with the full confidence that he would soon see Him whose presence was never absent.

His holiness and his humility were recognized both at the monastery and beyond it. His superior, Abbe Joseph de Beaufort, vicar general of Cardinal Louis Antoine de Noailles, came to him and learned from him. This worthy man later recalled these conversations and sought to put together with them the few scraps of writings and letters which Brother Lawrence had not destroyed. This effort resulted in the slim volume known as *The Practice of the Presence of God.*

PRAYER AND LIFE ARE ONE

"The time of business does not with me differ from the time of prayer, and in the noise and clatter of my kitchen, while several persons are calling for different things, I possess God in as great tranquility as if I were upon my knees at the Blessed Sacrament" (Brother Lawrence 1941).

Brother Lawrence believed that prayer and life are one. He looked upon his kitchen and business assignments as part of his religious life and discharged them accordingly. He saw it that way because for him prayer was being in the presence of God, not merely having one's mind filled with pious phrases. That was his fundamental message for all of us.

We might consider some assignments "unspiritual" or "beneath" the dignity of those who are described as spiritual giants. Brother Lawrence thought otherwise. On one occasion he speaks of a trip to buy wine in Burgundy. He did not consider himself to be a person who had "a turn for business," but this did not cause him uneasiness. He simply turned it over to God, saying that "it was His business he was about."

His candor and lack of false piety is also seen in his description of working in the monastery kitchen. He didn't really like such work. In fact, he had "a great aversion to it." But in spite of that he could say that "he had found everything easy in the fifteen years he had been employed there."

Brother Lawrence demonstrated how the Mary and Martha can live side by side in us. When we must endure the strain, drudgery, and even humiliation that can accompany our work, then the Martha in us will learn that it is important, even necessary to pray while cooking supper. Leaving behind mere talk about the dignity of labor, the Mary in us will learn what it takes to pray while standing at Martha's side (Luke 10:38–42).

O Lord, when we find ourselves in the frenzied and overheated kitchens of life, help us to carry on knowing that we are in your presence, called to do all things, great and small, to the glory of your name. Amen

PEACE THROUGH PARDON

Brother Lawrence had confessed to him, the Grand Vicar tells us, *"that when sometimes he had not thought of God for a good while, he did not disquiet himself for it; but after having acknowledged his wretchedness to God, he returned to Him with so much greater trust in Him as he had found himself wretched through forgetting Him"*(Brother Lawrence 1941).

Brother Lawrence once said that the practice of the presence of God is an easy thing to do. If this was all he said, we might resent him as one of those Christians who make everything sound so easy. For most of us it is not and, it seems, never will be. Least of all our prayers.

It is Brother Lawrence's willingness to be honest about himself and his failures. Why then should we be surprised that we, too, must confess that we are not yet perfectly trusting children of God who are always eager to commune with him? This is no reason to give up on ourselves and charge ourselves with unbelief. Unbelief is the refusal to turn to God.

We ought to be encouraged by our brother's report to the vicar that "when he failed in his duty, he simply confessed his fault, saying to God, 'I shall never do otherwise if Thou leavest me to myself; it is Thou who must hinder my failing, and mend what is amiss.' That after this he gave himself no further uneasiness about it. . . . That he was very sensible of his faults, but was not discouraged by them, that he confessed them to God, but did not plead against Him to excuse them. When he had so done, he peaceably resumed his usual practice of love and adoration" (Symons 1941).

As we consider these words we see that Brother Lawrence did not first of all see himself as an "achiever." Despite his years of cheerful service, despite his life of ceaseless prayer, he always saw himself as a recipient, receiving rest in the grace of God, free from worry, full of love.

O God, give us that understanding of ourselves which is both the counsel and the comfort of the Holy Spirit in your holy word. Amen

PRAYER IS LISTENING

Brother Lawrence told the Grand Vicar *"that his view of prayer was nothing but a sense of the Presence of God, his soul being at that time insensible to everything but Divine Love; and that when the appointed times of prayer were past, he found no difference, because he still continued with God, praising and blessing him with all his might, so that he passed his life in continual joy"* (Brother Lawrence 1941).

It doesn't take much to tempt us to give up on our prayers. Sometimes, when we hear the ardent prayer of others or read prayers which are beautiful, we are cast down. All we can perceive is our own inadequacy and inability to know how or what to ask. So, we think to ourselves, why bother at all? Such a sense of helplessness, however, may be the best thing that can happen to us, because now we are ready to turn to God in the one way that matters: giving over to Him everything.

In such a moment we may be most ready to understand the nature of Brother Lawrence's discovery about practicing the presence of God. He learned that prayer is more than words. Prayer involves waiting and often means closing our lips so that our Lord might have his turn to speak. It is a good thing to be silent at first, resting in the awareness that we are in the Lord's presence. It is the wise and mature Christian who knows how important it is to wait for the Father to speak. If we are willing to wait and be silent, we may find ourselves in conversations we never dreamed possible.

Such communion with God, Brother Lawrence says, cannot be shut off simply because one is done with formal prayer at a given hour. It is the joy of knowing that the Lord is going with you along the way. Who knows when he might not have another word to say?

Eternal Spirit of the living Christ,
I know not how to ask or what to say;
I only know my need, as deep as life,
And only you can teach me how to pray.
—*LBW* 441 (Frank von Christierson)

FAITH'S LOGIC

"How can we pray to Him without being with Him? How can we be with Him but in thinking of Him often? And how can we often think of Him unless by a holy habit of thought which we should form? You will tell me that I am always saying the same thing. It is true, for this is the best and easiest method I know; and as I use no other, I advise all the world to do it. We must know before we can love. In order to know God, we must often think of Him; and when we come to love Him, we shall then also think of Him often, for our heart will be with our treasure" (Brother Lawrence 1941).

Although he was hardly a trained theologian, Brother Lawrence speaks to us as a Sherlock Holmes of the seventeenth century as he answers, "Elementary, my dear Christian," and proceeds to tick off the steps in his logic: (1) To know God one must enter into a "holy habit of thought." (2) The more we then love, the more we will think of our Beloved. (3) Thus God will become more and more our treasure.

Brother Lawrence spoke much of experience, but he never separated experience from thought. He wrote in his very last letter, "And as knowledge is commonly the measure of love, the deeper and more extensive our knowledge shall be, the greater will be our *love:* and if our love of God be great, we shall love Him equally in grief and in joy" (Symons 1941).

Christian experience comes through knowledge which is incomplete without experience. Miriam Murphy writes, "Early Christians did not die in the Colosseum because they were expert theologians but because they knew him who dwelt within them and would overcome death."

May it be on our behalf that the Apostle prays, "that Christ may dwell in your hearts through faith; that you, being rooted and grounded in love, may have power to comprehend with all the saints what is the breadth and length and height and depth, and to know the love of Christ which surpasses knowledge, that you may be filled with all the fullness of God" (Eph. 3:17–19).

ALL FOR THE LOVE OF GOD

Brother Lawrence said *"that he found the best way of reaching God was by doing ordinary tasks, which he was obliged to perform under obedience, entirely for the love of God and not for the human attitude toward them"* (Brother Lawrence 1977).

We all know how easy it is to do the right thing for the wrong reason. Jesus spoke about this problem when he described the people who pray, give to charity, or engage in fasting, all for the same reason: to be seen by others. They have their reward, he said. They are seen by others.

The fault of such people seems so obvious that we overlook the more subtle ways in which we are subject to the same failing. Early on we learn that devotion to God and being helpful to others is one road to approval. We may also become people controlled by the expectations of others, filled with anxiety as we wonder what they might be thinking. From this anxiety it is but a short step to resentment as we begin to complain that people "don't appreciate how hard I am trying." Little wonder that for some, what passes for "religion" has become a state of bondage instead of the freedom which Christ came to bestow upon those who follow Him.

At this point, we would do well to turn to the apostolic invitation: "Whatever your task, work heartily, as serving the Lord and not men, knowing that from the Lord you will receive the inheritance as your reward; you are serving the Lord Christ" (Col. 3:23–24).

Paul is stating the simple truth that happiness rests in serving God, not in pursuing the approval of those around us. Peace comes when we are given a task to do, and we do it for him who is our companion, friend, and savior.

O Lord, grant that my life of Christian service will not become burned-out because I have forgotten my first love of You. Refresh and renew me through your love so that I may again put my whole heart into whatever You have given me to do. Amen

GOOD MEDICINE

"My good Mother: If we were accustomed to the regular exercise of the presence of God, all the ills of the body would be lessened; God often permits us to suffer a little to purify our souls and to bring us to him. . . . It grieves me to see you suffering so long; what lightens somewhat my sympathy for your suffering is that I am convinced it is proof of God's love for you" (Brother Lawrence 1977).

Brother Lawrence is full of surprises. He knew then what people today are hailing as a startling new discovery: the influence of a joyous spirit upon a physical malady. He joyfully proclaimed that the presence of God is good medicine, working wonders both spiritually and physically.

As the Proverbs remind us, "A merry heart doeth good like a medicine" (Prov. 17:22 KJV).

Brother Lawrence is not calling on us to deny the reality of pain or illness. He simply offers an antidote: "Love eases pain and when one loves God, one suffers for him with joy and courage." His only point is that it works wonders to adore God at all times, to trust in him without reservation, and to be assured of his unchanging love. I, too, have seen such holy laughter confound a pessimistic prognosis.

Trouble can become for us the anvil of God on which his Word strikes sparks as He says to us, "No, I won't let you go your own heedless way! Are you mine or not?" Through the Word we may then be led to say with renewed joy, "Yes, I do belong to God in the midst of this trouble. For in Jesus God has given us the promised Messiah who with us bears our griefs and carries our sorrows. It is he who has been bruised for our iniquities. By his stripes he brings healing to us all. Even in my troubles I am more than a conqueror through him who loves us" (compare Isa. 53:4–5; Rom. 8:37).

Heavenly Father, we need not deny our pain or our cause for sorrow, for we know you are with us and are filled with joy through the power of your presence. Amen

AN INTERIOR JOY

Brother Lawrence writes of himself, *"He is now so accustomed to this divine presence that he receives continual aid from it in all circumstances; for almost thirty years his soul has been filled with interior joys so continual and sometimes so great that to contain them and prevent their outward manifestation, he has resorted to behavior that seems more foolishness than piety"* (Brother Lawrence 1977).

Whence comes such joy as Brother Lawrence writes about? It comes out of union with Christ, a union we deepen through the practice of prayer. The aim of such prayer is not to make our Lord a push-button God who does what we say, but one in whom we live and who lives in us—a communion that is sacred, loving, joyful. We want the "love of God poured into our hearts through the Holy Spirit which has been given to us" (Rom. 5:5) not for selfish reasons, in the sense of personal glory, but for the sake of the self God sees as our potential.

One day a visitor stood on the coast of England and looked out over a vast stretch of mud in which ships tilted at crazy angles. He wondered what could be done. The heaving of an anchor or the hoisting of a sail would mean nothing. It was impossible to haul in enough water to fill the basin. Then, as he watched, the tide swept in. As the waters splashed against their side, the ships came to life again.

It is exactly in those moments when we feel we have been left totally "high and dry" that the flood tide of God's love can make us ready to sail again.

This is why Brother Lawrence would urge us to be open to and pray for the presence of God at all hours. Through communion with the Lord, the heart is delighted as in no other way.

Holy Spirit, through the knowledge of God's inexhaustible love fill me to the brim with your gift of joy. Amen

A LITTLE TALK WITH GOD

"It would be pertinent for those who undertake this practice to make up interiorly short ejaculations such as, 'My God, I am all yours,' 'God of love,' 'I love you with all my heart,' and any such words that love may beget on the spur of the moment." (Brother Lawrence 1977).

esus once spoke of people who would take the kingdom of God by violence. Many of us would seize it and conquer it through our knowledge and ability to use words. We meditate on what we read and hear. We take notes. But there is another way. It is something more intuitive. A friend has put the formula this way: "Rest in God as He rests in you." She calls for a time of quiet and listening. We need a time of waiting for God's response as we give ourselves over to quietness.

Through a simple resting in God, growth comes as growth always must come: slowly. If a wound heals best when it heals slowly, and if only slowly does the seed grow and mature into a beautiful tree, then why think that the beauty of God's holiness can be attained through a religious cram course? As Brother Lawrence, with a trace of humor, says of Sister N——, "She appears to me to be full of good will, but she wants to go faster than grace. One does not become holy all at once."

O Lord, help us to encourage one another, to forgive one another, to be patient with one another, and to delight in one another, to the end that we might help each other into a deeper communion with You, the source of every good gift. Amen

WHO SHALL SEE GOD?

"By the presence of God and by this interior gaze, the soul comes to know God in such a way that it is . . . always engaged in this divine presence" (Brother Lawrence 1977).

Can a mortal human being see God? Moses asked to see him, but was denied, except for a glimpse of the Lord's departing glory. Furthermore, the Gospel has declared, "No one has ever seen God" (John 1:18). If we are speaking of a visual record received by the retina, most certainly it is impossible to see God.

And yet, seeing not, we see God another way. We see Him by faith. We behold Him through what Brother Lawrence describes as the soul's "interior gaze." It is a seeing just as real as anything caught by the mechanism of the eye and brain.

This is the vision which is promised in our Lord's beatitude spoken in the Sermon on the Mount. He speaks of the "pure in heart," the people who "shall see God." While the absolute and total fulfillment of Jesus' promise shall take place only at the end of time, it shall also happen as we turn to him with unquestioning obedience and heartfelt adoration. It is then that, seeing not, we see.

We only know that at the end, as Joseph Sittler suggests, this seeing certainly will *not* be the discovery that God looks like us, only on a much grander scale. Such a claim would be both blasphemy against God and idolatry of mankind.

What we shall see goes beyond the limits of human language. We simply know that we will see God as his glory becomes our light and his presence our life. In the meantime, through the Father's disclosure of himself in his only Son, through this act of sheer grace, we are able to pray,

O my soul,
Why these eyes shut so tight?
Open them now and thus begin
To see Him who will be your Light
Through all your days in heaven.

CENTERING ON GOD

"I cannot imagine how religious persons can live satisfied without the practice of the presence of God. For my part, I keep myself retired with Him in the very center of my soul as much as I can; and while I am so with Him, I fear nothing" (Brother Lawrence 1941).

As we leave Brother Lawrence, let us remember that he was not out to foster one particular "method" of devotional life. Only one thing really mattered to him: seeking the presence of God. Concerning this goal, he would not tolerate indifference.

Brother Lawrence reminds us that our goal will not take place by our talking about prayer, but only by the *doing* of it. To that end, the following exercises may help us to center on God and enter into communion with God:

Sit back in a relaxed manner, your back straight and both feet on the floor, your whole body as relaxed as possible, leaving your soul free. Thank and praise God for all he has done through the day.

Reflect for a moment on a passage of Scripture.

Concentrate your consciousness on the loving presence of Christ within your inner self. Think of how much you love and honor him. Exclude other thoughts as best you can. "Seek the things that are above, where Christ is, seated at the right hand of God" (Col. 3:1).

Breathe deeply and rhythmically, for this in itself brings calm and peace. Speak softly the names of the Lord. Say little things such as, "My God, I am all yours," "God of love, I love you with all my heart," "My Lord and my God, heal me and free me."

As you are relaxed and centering on the presence of God within you, you may wish to make use of a favorite and simple prayer. It may simply be the doxology or a prayer to the Lamb of God who takes away the sins of the world.

Then, whether it is in such a moment set apart, or in the newly found peace that attends our given tasks, our life becomes this prayer: Whether we sleep or wake, work or play, may we ever know, O Lord, "the mystery hidden for ages . . . but now made manifest to his saints . . . which is Christ in you, the hope of glory" (Col. 1:26–27).

JOHN BUNYAN

Durwood Buchheim

JOHN BUNYAN (1628–1688), SON OF THOMAS BUNYAN JR. AND Margaret Bentley, was born in the heart of the English midlands. He was to spend all of his life in this small, rural village of Elstow, which was next door to Bedford. John grew up in a poor, humble home. He who was to become a world-renowned author attended elementary school for about two years. At the age of 16, he joined the army of the Parliament fighting for the cause of liberty against the troops of the Government. His military adventure was more family than politically motivated. John Bunyan joined the army to get away from home!

Returning from the army, and becoming a tinker, a brazier, a traveling fixer and seller of pots and pans, John married the daughter of a devout Protestant. John said this about his marriage, "Until I came to the state of marriage, I was the very ringleader in all manner of vice and ungodliness." John's wife gave him a good push toward maturity. During these years his life was like a "seesaw" between hope and despair. During this time the Bible and Luther's commentary on Galatians prepared him for baptism. At the age of twenty-five he was baptized and joined the Baptist Church in Bedford. He was to remain a member of that church all his life—serving as deacon, lay preacher, and pastor.

In 1660 he was arrested and the next twelve years of his life were spent in prison. But jail did not dampen his spirit nor weaken his devotion to ministry. From prison he sent forth book after book, all of which demonstrated remarkable knowledge of the Bible.

In 1672 John Bunyan was set free. He became the preacher/pastor of the Bedford congregation. In this small, simple place John Bunyan became the focus of a renewal movement and the rallying place for growing crowds of worshipers. He attracted people with his zeal, wit, and insight. He had a great sense of humor. He preached and ministered to all people with great passion and compassion. On a forty-mile trip to London he was drenched and chilled by a driving rainstorm. He caught a fever and, at the age of sixty, died.

THESE WORDS UPON YOUR HEART

"Read, and read again, and do not despair of help to understand something of the will and mind of God, though you think they are fast locked up from you. Neither trouble your heads though you have not commentaries and expositions; pray and read, and read and pray. . . . There is nothing that so abides with us as what we receive from God. . . . Things that we receive at God's hand come to us as things from the minting-house, though old in themselves, yet new to us. Old truths are always new to us, if they come to us with the smell of heaven upon them" (Bunyan 1952).

It is through words that we are encountered by God. This is what we mean when we say, "the Word of God is a means of grace." It is the means, the way, the method through which God meets us. God is revealed to us through human language.

So, early in the Bible we read these words from Moses, "And these words which I command you this day shall be upon your heart; and you shall teach them diligently to your children, and shall talk of them when you sit in your house, and when you walk by the way, and when you lie down, and when you rise" (Deut. 6:6–7).

"These words upon your heart" are the most valuable heritage the chosen people of God had. Virtually every crisis that God's people faced, the word of God was there to provide a lamp for the feet and light for the path.

Luke, the author of the Book of Acts, tells us that missionary Paul "argued with the people from the scriptures . . . explaining and proving that it was necessary for the Christ to suffer and to rise from the dead." It was in this congregation that Paul and Silas were described in those never-to-be-forgotten words: "These men, who have turned the world upside down, have come here also" (Acts 17:6).

"Read and read again. . . ." This counsel by Bunyan remains timely and on target. We have good intentions, but it seems we make little progress. Don't despair. Don't quit. Your reading of this devotional book may mark a new beginning of Bible reading for you.

Read Deuteronomy 6:1–9 and Acts 17.

THE THRONE OF GRACE

"Grace can pardon our ungodliness and justify us with Christ's righteousness; it can put the Spirit of Jesus Christ within us; it can help us when we are down; it can heal us when we are wounded; it can multiply pardons as we through frailty multiply transgressions" (Bunyan 1952).

Somewhere I read the great twentieth-century theologian Karl Barth said something like this: "God's judgment doesn't bother us, we can handle that. But God's grace, that scares the devil out of us." It is hard for us to believe that God loves sinners while they are still sinners! It just doesn't make sense.

For me and for many others, the most beautiful picture of grace in all of Scriptures is the father welcoming home his young son. We hear that the father does not wait for the son, but runs to meet him. And he doesn't even permit this wasteful rascal to finish his confession. He chokes it off with a big bear hug and then calls for the ring, the shoes, and the robe, all powerful symbols of instant restoration to the family. In this memorable homecoming we see the sheer goodness of God.

Bunyan experienced God's grace. He entitled his spiritual biography, *Grace Abounding to the Chief of Sinners.* This is one of his definitions of grace: "But do thou remember that the grace of God is his good-will and great love to sinners, in his Son Jesus Christ." He also compares the grace of God to a river: "so those who live by grace are compared to fish; for that, as water is that element in which the fish lives, so grace is that which is the life of the saint."

Jesus' great parable of the prodigal son was directed to people who were offended at the gospel. We may have a similar problem. Thus the story of the loving father becomes the story for repentant young people who are wasting their lives in "riotous living." The elder brother is a powerful witness to the fact that one doesn't even have to leave home to be far from the father. "The far country," writes Augustine, "is forgetfulness of God." But God loves us even in the far country.

Read Luke 15.

GRACE OF FEAR

"It seems to me as if this grace of fear was the darling grace, the grace that God set his heart upon at the highest rate. . . .This grace of fear is the soft-est and most tender of God's honor of all the graces. . . .We cannot watch as we should, if we are destitute of fear. . . .This grace of fear can make the man that in many other things is not capable of serving God, serve him better than those that have all else without it" (Bunyan 1952).

One wonders if we who have developed such a cozy familiarity with the Almighty can have any appreciation for Bunyan's "grace of fear." I read somewhere that Isaiah's tormented cry, "I'm of unclean lips and I dwell in the midst of a people of unclean lips," has been replaced by the comfortable, popular response, "Lord, I do the best I can, you know . . . you know. After all you don't expect us to be perfect, do you?" C. S. Lewis called this a "flabby kind" of religion, and so it is.

But the other side of that observation is that many of us desire something more substantial in our relationship with God than someone whom we can manipulate. Is there any way we can restore the tension between the lowly Lord who is our pal and the High and Holy One who is our Lord?

Maybe a beginning could be made if we would look more kindly on the word *fear* (or reverence, which is its basic meaning). Luther reminds us in the Small Catechism that the true interpretation of the First and chief Commandment, "Thou shall have no other gods before me," means simply this: "Thou shalt fear, love, and trust in God above everything else." It is Luther's contention that the Bible gives emphasis to these two points—fear of and trust in God.

Bunyan speaks of the "grace of fear." He also describes the "fear of the Lord as the pulse of the soul." So he urges us to pray, "Lord, unite my heart to fear thy name, and do not harden mine heart from thy fear."

Read Genesis 28:10–17 and Luke 9:28–36.

FEAR NEED NOT OWN US

"There are but few when they come to the cross, say Welcome, cross! as some of the martyrs did to the stake they were burned at. Therefore, if you meet with the cross in thy journey, be not daunted and say, what shall I do now? but rather take courage, knowing that by the cross is the way to the kingdom." (Bunyan 1952).

There is fear afoot in our world, but it is not the fear of God. Death has always been a great fear, but in our time that is in danger of being replaced by our fear of living. Fear is reshaping the center and focus of our lives. It intensifies the greed in us. Fear empowers the arms race. Our massive military preparations to avoid war are making us prisoners of our own fears. Bunyan's character "Mr. Fearing" is insightful at this point: *"Mr. Fearing was one that played upon the bass. For my part, I care not at all for that profession that begins not in heaviness of mind. The first string that the musician usually touches is the bass, when he intends to put all in tune; God also plays upon this string first, when he set the soul in tune for himself. Only, there was the imperfection of Mr. Fearing, he could play upon no other music but this till toward his latter end."*

James Forest tells the story of young Mel Hollander who received the very bad news that he was dying of cancer and at the most had six months to live. He heard of a course at Union Theological Seminary for those who would be working with the dying. Mel registered for it and also for a course on the book of Revelation being taught by Daniel Berrigan. At the opening of Berrigan's class Mel was quite nervous. He was aware of his physical condition and fearful of what other people might say. Teacher Berrigan focused on him and asked: "What's the matter?" Mel, thinking the question was rude, responded: "I'm dying of cancer." There was brief pause and then Berrigan's response: "That must be very exciting." It was the moment of transfiguration for Mel. It wasn't that he was no longer fearful, but fear no longer owned him. (*Sojourners*, February 1980).

Read Romans 8:31–39.

LIFE IN THE WILDERNESS

"The school of the cross is the school of light: it discovers the world's vanity, baseness, and wickedness, and lets us see more of God's mind. Out of dark afflictions comes a spiritual light" (Bunyan 1952).

For most of chapter 15 in the book of Exodus, the children of Israel have a good time celebrating. But then they are in the wilderness. And it is not like our protected wilderness areas. No, the wilderness was a lonely place full of fear, danger, and suffering. The people of God became thirsty, hungry, and lost. They wanted to go back to Egypt, but instead spent forty years in the wilderness—as long as most of our careers.

Jesus had just been baptized. He heard the promise: "You are my beloved son in whom I am well pleased." The first result of that promise was trouble. The same Spirit who called him "beloved" now ordered him into the wilderness to be tested by the Evil One. As Israel, the old "Son of God," was tested through forty years in the wilderness, so also there was struggle and testing for Jesus Christ. Jesus went from the mountain on Sunday to the wilderness on Monday.

Because he persisted in preaching the word of God, which was contrary to the laws of the state, Bunyan was arrested and put into the county jail of Bedford. This was no modern prison, but a place of stench and dirt. The best part of Bunyan's life was spent in this place. The prisoner saw his suffering as an opportunity that might stir up "the saints in the country" to renewed dedication and faithfulness.

We like to think that life in Christ is an escape from wilderness living. Sometimes that is how the faith is proclaimed—salvation is equated with the American Dream. But that is an illusion. Though our testing experiences may not be as severe as they were for Jesus or Bunyan (if we lived in South Africa, it would be different!), there is no way back to Egypt or forward to the promised land except through the wilderness.

The testing in the wilderness reveals what we are made of. The journey continues. But it continues with our Lord who in all ways was tested as we are.

HOPE HAS A THICK SKIN

"Despair undervalues the promise, undervalues the invitation, undervalues the offer of grace. Despair undervalues the ability of God the Father, and the redeeming blood of Christ his Son. Oh, unreasonable despair"(Bunyan 1952).

Our century began in an "orgy of optimism." That optimism died with World War One—one of the most horrendous wars in history. In its wake, we feel we are left only with despair; as Henri Nouwen writes: "[We live in] a world clouded with an all-pervading fear, a growing sense of despair, and the paralyzing awareness that humanity has come to the verge of suicide."

In order not to despair, we may turn to either of two extremes. One is called cynicism. It seeks to save people from their own expectations. Today cynicism is being replaced by narcissism. Our cynics want to be left alone to enjoy themselves. On the other side of the fence we have the "credulous ones," shutting their eyes to the real world. One believes in believing, no matter the evidence to the contrary. One's expectations are guided by unquestioned assumptions.

So it is hard not to despair. Bunyan indicates his personal struggle with despair in these words, "I would say to my soul, this is not the place of despair; this is not the time to despair in. . . . As long as there is a moment left in me of breath or life in this world, so long will I fight against unbelief and despair."

It is our faith that holds together both expectation and experience. The focal point of that tension is the cross of Jesus Christ. Faith doesn't lie about the world and will accept the struggle. It is in continual dialogue with its constant shadow—doubt. But in the struggle, faith does not give up on the promise.

Herein is our hope. "Faith is the assurance of things hoped for, the conviction of things not seen" (Heb. 11:1). Hope is faith fulfilled in the future. Preacher Bunyan writes: "Faith says to hope, Look for what is promised. Hope says to faith, so I do, and will wait for it too. Hope has a thick skin and will endure many a blow."

Read Romans 5:1–5 and 8:18–30.

LOVING GOD WITH OUR MIND

"The greatest part of professors nowadays take up their time in contracting guilt and asking for pardon, and yet are not much the better. Whereas, if they had but the grace to add to their faith, virtue, etc., they might have more peace, live better lives and not have their heads so often in a bag, as they have"(Bunyan 1952).

An outspoken individual, Daniel Webster said, "Education can make us into clever devils." Bunyan would have agreed. Of keen mind and good judgment, he seemed to be unduly suspicious of formal education. He read few books and justified his ignorance because it permitted the Spirit to work unhindered.

There is an old story about an airline pilot that goes like this: after the plane had gone through a terrible storm the pilot said to the passengers, "I'm sorry about the rough ride, but there wasn't much I could do about it. I think we are through the worst of it, although there are still a few problems. We have lost our navigational equipment. It appears that we are lost, but I want you to know that we are making good time."

"It appears that we are lost, but we are making good time," could well be the epitaph of our century. Clever devils are more concerned with ends than with the means to an end. Their first question is not: "Is this the right thing to do?" but rather, "Is this going to be effective?" This provokes the need for education to produce *wise saints,* not clever devils.

Of course we are not saved by our education. But neither does salvation place a premium on ignorance. To the woman of Samaria Christ said, "You worship what you do not know" (John 4:22). Too many of us are in that predicament today, fumbling and groping in a kind of theological fog with inaccurate compasses making us vulnerable to clever devils.

The great commandment reminds us to not only love God with our whole heart and soul, but also with our mind.

Read Matthew 22:34–40 and Ephesians 4:11–15.

WHO SPEAKS FOR THE POOR?

"There are two sorts of good works; and a man may be shrewdly guessed at with reference to his faith, even by the works that he chooses to be conversant in. There are works that cost nothing, and works that are chargeable; and observe it, the unsound faith will choose to itself the most easy works it can find: for example, there is reading, praying, hearing of sermons, baptism, breaking of bread, church-fellowship, preaching, and the like; and there is mortification of lusts, charity, simplicity, and open-heartedness with a liberal hand to the poor, and their like also" (Bunyan 1952).

I t has been pointed out that the most pessimistic statement Jesus made is his conclusion of the uncomfortable Rich Man/Poor Man story: "If they do not hear Moses and the prophets, neither will they be convinced if someone should rise from the dead" (Luke 16:31).

The rich man and the poor man die. But here is the great reversal. The rich man ends up in hell and the poor man is safe in the arms of Abraham. In many of Jesus' parables, the real point is revealed in the last sentence. The point of this story is the massive indifference and apathy on the part of the rich in regard to the poor. The real issue is not inequality, but inequality coupled with indifference. If the rich do not learn sympathy with the Bible in their hands and Lazarus at their gates, not even a voice from the dead will convince them.

Bunyan was a noteworthy example in his day, speaking for the poor, even remaining poor despite the income from the sale of his books. Who speaks for the poor today? Aren't we Christians supposed to have some equipment that helps us understand the tragedy of poverty? I don't have the answer to poverty but would suggest that we who follow the Lord Christ could begin by speaking and standing for the poor.

Read Jeremiah 13–17 and Luke 16:19–31.

Going Home in the Arms
of the Savior

"It was not the overheavy Load of Sin, but the Discovery of Mercy; not the Roaring of the Devil, but the Drawing of the Father, that makes a Person come to Jesus Christ: I myself know all of these Things" (Bunyan 1952).

A well-known parable by Jesus is usually called the story of the "lost sheep." We didn't raise sheep on the farm where I grew up. My dad regarded them as stupid, stubborn, and prone to mysterious diseases. Taking care of sheep was too frustrating and wasn't worth the time and effort.

I would like to suggest that the emphasis of our text is not upon sheep, but upon the shepherd. Neither is badness nor goodness the point of this story. This story is not about a repentant or sorry sheep searching for its master. It's the other way around. The shepherd searches for the lost sheep "till he finds it." But even finding the lost one does not end the shepherd's task. No, now the shepherd must carry the lost one home. This story is about restoration.

Bunyan had a sensitive conscience and an active imagination. This combination created for him terrifying images and visions of the oncoming day of judgment. It was during these stormy years that he read Luther's commentary on Paul's epistle to the Galatians. This was one of the experiences whereby he was found by God. Years later he was to write his most important book, *Pilgrim's Progress,* and its opening sentence is quite revealing: "As I walked through the wilderness of this world . . ."

It is hard not to get lost in the wilderness of this world. Our congregations are made up of people who are both shepherds and sheep. You and I are a mixture of being lost and found. Ours is not an "I found it" faith. It is just the opposite. We have a God who doesn't calculate the cost in searching for and finding us. Thanks be to God! We are in the arms of the Savior, going home!

Read Luke 15:1—7.

THE RESURRECTION

(John Bunyan died in London, after traveling there to bring about a reconciliation between a father and his son. He was buried in Bunhill Fields, Finsbury.) *"The doctrine of the resurrection, however questioned by heretics and erroneous persons, yet is such a truth, that almost all the holy scriptures of God point at and center in it"* (Bunyan 1952).

Theologian Joseph Sittler was convinced that "the fear of death is at the bottom of all apprehensions." History has recorded many great events, but there can be little question that the greatest is the resurrection of Jesus Christ. It has been called "history's turning point."

The resurrection event has been the focus of much controversy and many explanations. The much debated question is, "Did the empty tomb create the Easter faith or did the Easter faith create the empty tomb?" If you spend much time reading the various biblical accounts of the resurrection you will discover there are disagreements in the descriptions of what happened.

"He is not here. He is risen." According to Mark's account the empty tomb did not initially create faith and understanding, but rather fear and terror. The resurrection is something that happened between Jesus and God and not God and the disciples. What can be historically verified at the death of Jesus is the death of Jesus. Later, after some time of reflection and prayer, there was the great resurgence of power and hope in the words and deeds of the early followers of Christ. Jesus' empty tomb is the focus and source of that hope and power.

I believe in the promise of the resurrection because of the biblical witness of the empty tomb and its results. I also believe in the resurrection because a God who loves us so much as to die for us is not going to be frustrated by death. In the Bible, the power of death comes under the control of God. With the apostle Paul, I confess, "If we live, we live to the Lord, and if we die, we die to the Lord; so then, whether we live or die, we are the Lord's" (Rom. 14:7–8).

Read Luke 24, Matthew 28:1–10, and Mark 16.

SØREN KIERKEGAARD

Edna and Howard Hong

EVERYONE, FROM GRADUATE STUDENTS AND JOURNALISTS TO theologians and philosophers, is dropping the name Søren Kierkegaard these days. Major journals of philosophy, religion, or psychology that do not contain his name are rare. One is tempted to ask: Are people merely name-dropping or is this man actually that important?

To the country (Denmark) and century (1813–1855) in which Kierkegaard lived, he was decidedly unimportant, and outside of Scandinavia was practically unknown. In this century the whole world considers him to have had and to have as much influence on contemporary thought as any other thinker of either his century or ours.

A century and a half ago Kierkegaard was grappling with the very issues that plague the modern conscience. Indeed, he predicted very precisely in his writings the dehumanization that has happened and is happening in this secular, materialistic society. No physician has ever diagnosed a disease more perceptibly than Kierkegaard has diagnosed the human condition. No preacher of penitence has described more honestly and devastatingly than he the consequences of the loss of self in the denial of God.

"What does it mean to exist?" Kierkegaard asked, using the word in its original Latin meaning, to stand forth, to live a life that is more than we mean when we say, "merely existing." But then he loads the phrase "to exist" with his own meaning—namely, to exist in what one understands, to exist in the truth one understands. For Kierkegaard, truth is not a matter only of knowing but of being. It is a life.

Kierkegaard also wrote out of the old-fashioned, orthodox Christian faith. For him, Christ was the truth, and to exist in the truth meant to follow Christ, to deny oneself, and to walk the same way as Christ walked in the humble form of a servant. This poses a special problem for Lutherans. The Lutheran principle of grace alone, faith alone, and Christ as gift has often meant that following Christ, the imitation of Christ, and good works have fallen by the wayside. But it is demoralizing, maintains Kierkegaard, to receive Christ only as gift. Indeed, has one received the gift if there is no response?

Thus Kierkegaard saw himself as a missionary, not to pagans, but to Christians! He perceived his mission to be to reintroduce Christianity into Christendom.

86

MY HIGHEST PERFECTION

"To need God is man's highest perfection. . . . Man's highest achievement is to let God be able to help him" (Kierkegaard 1967).

o need, to be needy, to be in any kind of extremity is not something desirable in this day and age. If it is at all avoidable, one is expected to escape need by any and every possible route. Feel good about yourself. If we do not "feel comfortable" with something, we shun it. The primary aim of the burgeoning business of counseling is to create a sense of well-being in those who come seeking advice. Even the church, says Kierkegaard, has become trendy and presents Christianity *"in a certain almost enervated form of coddling love. It is always love, love; spare yourself and your flesh and blood; have pleasant days or delightful days without self-made cares, for God is love, love—of strenuousness nothing must be heard . . ."* (Kierkegaard 1962).

"The method now," wrote Kierkegaard in his journals, *"is to leave out the existentially strenuous passages in the New Testament. We hush them up—and then we arrange things on easier and cheaper terms. We probably think that since we did not mention these passages God does not know that they are in the New Testament"* (Kierkegaard 1967).

No Christian would recommend hushing up the good news of our soul's salvation through Jesus Christ, but ought the church hush the bad news of the human condition that makes us desperately need God? Furthermore, ought we not assume that the Father is like the Son and is most accepting and welcoming to the person who is most in need and knows it? Indeed, says Kierkegaard, more pleasing to God than hymn singing is a human being who genuinely feels that he or she needs him. With such a person God wants to and can communicate and help.

"God in heaven, let me rightly feel my nothingness, not to despair over it, but all the more intensely to feel the greatness of your goodness" (Kierkegaard 1967).

'TIS I, I WHO NEED GOD!

"Christianity is not at all right to stress that all humankind needs Christianity and then to prove it and demonstrate it. The Christian stress is: I need Christianity" (Kierkegaard 1967).

I t is not society, my generation, my community, my church, my friends—it is *I* who need the relationship to God that Christianity proclaims is available to me in Jesus Christ. By disobedience the human race fell into sin and out of relationship to God, but by Christ's obedience the human race was not restored en masse to relationship to God. That amazing grace is offered to and received not by they's or we's, but by individuals, by I's. God needs and wants to relate to and to communicate to I's, and the I most welcome to him is the I who needs him most. God's ear is open to the I who says to him, "I need you, oh, I need you! Every hour I need you!"

A relationship such as that is a firsthand relationship, not second- or thirdhand. "A secondhand relationship to God," says Kierkegaard, "is just as impossible and just as nonsensical as falling in love at second hand." If I forget the price that Christ paid so that I can have a firsthand relationship to God and believe the cost for me is too high, there is no place where I can buy, beg, or borrow a secondhand relationship. One can be brought to God through the intimate relationship to God of parents, of a spouse, of a friend, but one cannot ride tandem into that relationship with them. God requires of you and me an original, direct, firsthand relationship. Only as an I, an I who needs God and knows that I need God, can I truly relate to him.

My Father in heaven, I know very well that you know that I need you. You do not need to hear me say it, but you want to hear me say it and I need to say it. Thank you for being that concerned with me that you want to hear me tell you my need of you. Amen

Baptism Is No Insurance Policy

"If people absolutely insist on infant baptism, then they ought all the more vigorously see to it that rebirth becomes a decisive determinant in becoming a Christian" (Kierkegaard 1967).

By no means does Kierkegaard deny or minimize the effect or benefit of baptism. He believes with Luther that "in baptism God forgives sin, delivers from death and the devil, and gives everlasting salvation to all who believe what he has promised" (The Small Catechism). He also believes with Luther that "it is not water that does these things but God's word with the water and our trust in this word. Water by itself is only water, but with this word it is a life-giving water which by grace gives the new birth through the Holy Spirit."

Neither does Kierkegaard question infant baptism, but he has serious concerns about any mistaken view that infant baptism takes care of everything. What Kierkegaard questions is making infant baptism an insurance policy, a guarantee of salvation. He challenges being so secure and unconcerned about infant baptism that it can become what he calls "an ungodly flippancy."

I was born a sinner, but I was not born twenty or thirty years old, an adult who is conscious of my sin. I was born a baby Adam or a baby Eve. In baptism I was reborn and received a new quality. I became a new Adam or a new Eve. I was not conscious of the total qualitative transformation that took place in me in my baptism—a change that is just as totally qualitative, says Kierkegaard, "as the change from not being to being, which is birth." That consciousness is an adult consciousness. Growing into what I was made in baptism is an adult task, my lifetime task.

"Do you not know that all of us who have been baptized into Christ Jesus were baptized into his death? We were buried therefore with him by baptism into death, so that as Christ was raised from the dead by the glory of the Father, we too might walk in newness of life" (Rom. 6:3–5).

GRACE FIRST AND LAST

"What does Christ require? First and foremost, faith. Next, gratitude. In the disciple in the stricter sense this gratitude is 'imitation.' But even the weakest Christian has this in common with the strongest disciple: the relationship is one of gratitude. Imitation is not a requirement of the law, for then we have the system of law again. No, imitation is the stronger expression of gratitude in the stronger" (Kierkegaard 1967).

f Kierkegaard did nothing else, he set Christian concepts in their proper order. However acrid he at times makes being a Christian taste, he always comes back to grace—first, last, and always, faith in God's grace. Although he accuses Luther of easing up on imitation, he credits him with the right order, but adds his own corrective: *"Luther rightly orders it this way. Christ is the gift—to which faith corresponds. Then he is the pattern, the*

90

prototype to which imitation corresponds. Still more accurately one may say: (1) imitation in the direction of decisive action, whereby the situation for becoming a Christian comes into existence; (2) Christ as gift—faith; (3) imitation as the fruit of faith"(Kierkegaard 1967).

Luther lived in a time when the order was reversed and Christ as pattern or prototype was placed above Christ as gift. If there is no requirement, there is no guilt. If there is no guilt, who needs grace? If there is no need for grace, grace is taken for granted and there is no gratitude. If Kierkegaard was scandalized by the confusion and disorder and dilution of Christian categories in his day, what would he think today, in this day of "gratitude for what? Everything I've got, I have coming to me! They are my rights, and if I don't get my rights, I'll sue anyone and even you to get them!"

"O, infinite grace, have mercy on me for being here again so soon and having to plead for grace, for now I understand that in order to have peace and rest, in order not to perish in hopeless despair, in order to be able to breathe, in order to be able to exist at all, I need grace not only for the past but grace for the future" (Kierkegaard 1967).

THE DIALECTIC OF FAITH

"It is clear that in my writings I have supplied a more radical characteriza-
tion of the concept of 'faith' than there has been up until this time"
(Kierkegaard 1967).

If Kierkegaard's characterization of faith is radical, it is
because it is dialectical. *Dialectical* means that there is
more than one side to most things. This makes possible
movement back and forth—in other words, dialogue.

Faith, says Kierkegaard, is dialectical, and the tragedy of
Christendom is that we have removed the dialectical element. We
make faith one-sided by defining it as merely hoping against hope
and believing against understanding. If faith becomes static, cozy,
or secure, then, says Kierkegaard, faith is in grave danger.

Kierkegaard adds to the definition of faith the tension of will,
of choice, of obedience. I am not to insist on proofs of the existence of God and then believe. I move on from the understanding
that faith cannot be understood to the understanding that faith *must*
not be understood. I choose to believe, I make the leap of faith, I
will to venture my whole life on Christ's *if:* "If you continue in my
word, you are truly my disciples" (John 8:31).

The dialectical movement of faith is from believing to striving
and back to faith. *"Luther is completely right in saying that if a man had to*
acquire his salvation by his own striving, it would end either in presumption
or despair, and therefore it is faith that saves. But yet not in such a way that
striving vanishes completely. Faith should make striving possible, because the
fact that I am saved by faith and that nothing at all is demanded from me
should in itself make it possible that I begin to strive, that I do not collapse
under impossibility but am encouraged and refreshed, because it has been
decided I am saved, I am God's child by virtue of faith" (Kierkegaard 1967).

"For by grace you have been saved through faith; and this is not your own
doing, it is the gift of God—not because of works, lest any man should boast.
For we are his workmanship, created in Jesus Christ for good works, which God
prepared beforehand, that we should walk in them"(Eph. 2:8–10).

KIERKEGAARD DEFINES CHRISTIANITY

"Christianly, the emphasis does not fall so much upon to what extent or how far a person succeeds in meeting or fulfilling the requirement, if he actually is striving, as it is upon his getting an impression of the requirement in all its infinitude so that he rightly learns to be humbled and to rely upon grace. To pare down the requirement in order to fulfill it better . . . to this Christianity in its deepest essence is opposed. No, infinite humiliation and grace, and then a striving born of gratitude—this is Christianity" (Kierkegaard 1967).

bout this time someone may well sputter in protest: "Listen! You can't talk out of two sides of your mouth—is that what you mean by being dialectical? You can't talk about being saved by faith, about nothing at all being demanded, and then start yammering about striving to fulfill a requirement!"

No, we are not making grace into a new law, and neither did Kierkegaard. The requirement is the "for what?" that follows as a matter of course after faith. I am saved by faith. For what? Why, of course, to express my faith in my daily life! Grace is God's gift to me, and he gave it to me with the intention of transforming me. His hope is that I will respond to his gift by choosing to strive to obey his word and his will as revealed by his son Jesus Christ and by his apostles. I don't have to look long and hard to find his word and will—it's on every page of the New Testament.

Kierkegaard speaks scathingly about paring down the Christian requirement or suppressing it in order to make following it easy. This, he says, is taking grace in vain. The purpose of the requirement is not to make us torment ourselves or to judge others for not expressing faith in their lives. It is to humble us before its infinite demand and send us to grace—and then in gratitude for grace return again to the striving to follow and obey.

Christ, my Redeemer, teach me to thank you in the only way you want, the way of following you and obeying you. And when I flub and fail and fall flat on my face, forgive me, pick me up, and set me to striving in gratitude again. Amen

CHRIST AS THE SIGN OF OFFENSE

*"Since Holy Scripture says 'Woe to the men by whom the temptation comes,'
we confidently say: Woe to him who first thought of preaching Christianity
without the possibility of offense. . . . Woe to the person who betrayed and
broke the mystery of faith, distorted it into public wisdom, because he took
away the possibility of offense! Woe to the person who could comprehend the
mystery of atonement without detecting anything of the possibility of
offense"* (Kierkegaard 1962).

 ow in the world, asked Kierkegaard 150 years ago, could
anyone be offended by modern Christianity? Even then he
could see the cultural accommodation that was taking
place in the established Church and could see that it was no longer
proclaiming Christ as the sign of contradiction. He could see that it
no longer was preaching Christ as a scandal to the world and to our
human nature. He could foresee that if Christ is not proclaimed so
that one is either offended by him or believes in him, then
Christianity is bound to decline, people will become bored with the
church or drop out. Then Christianity is as good as abolished and
the churches might as well be locked up.

93

Are you perhaps thinking "What outrageous thoughts! That
Kierkegaard must be a fanatic!" So you are offended! Good! Then you
are in the situation where you must bring Christ out of history into
this very present moment, must make him contemporary with you
here on the spot and reflect on what he is saying to you here and now.

Jesus said to John's disciples, "Blessed is he who takes no
offense at me" (Matt. 11:6). Christ clearly sees the possibility of
offense in himself, and just as clearly is offended by our not per-
ceiving it. To perceive it—and then believe—ah, then Christ can
be sure that he has an invincible follower!

*Christ Jesus, your most potent missionary, Paul, was so offended by you that he
threatened to slaughter your followers. You had to give him a blinding vision of
yourself before he could believe. If my faith is so insipid that it offends you, do
not spew me out of your mouth but let your Holy Spirit shake salt into it! Amen*

THE PROOF OF FAITH AND LOVE

"'He who sees his brother in need, yet shuts his heart' (1 John 3:17)—yes, at the same time he shuts God out. Love to God and love to neighbor are like two doors that open simultaneously, so that it is impossible to open one without opening the other, and impossible to shut one without shutting the other" (Kierkegaard 1967).

 aith is known by love, and love is not a feeling but works of love. The proof of faith and love, is not in the language of words but in the language of works in love, *"Christ's love was not intense feeling, a full heart, etc.; it was rather the works of love, which is his life"* (Kierkegaard 1967).

So often we say, "It would have been so easy to show my faith and love if I had been contemporary with Christ." Ah, but we are contemporary with the sick, the poor, the despised, the suffering. As reported by Matthew, Christ made it clear that if we do works of love to the "least of these" we do them to him (Matt. 25:31–46).

The Great Commandment, the one Christ calls "the great and first commandment" (Matt. 22:37–38) says: "You shall love the Lord your God with all your heart, and with all your soul, and with all your mind." Kierkegaard points out that it does not say "You shall love God as you love yourself." Christ pinned that phrase to the Second Commandment: "You shall love your neighbor as yourself." That little phrase "as yourself" causes us to think and struggle with what it means to love ourselves; in the struggle we learn to love ourselves in the proper way so that we can love the neighbor as ourselves. Moreover, Christ makes love to the neighbor a divine command, a divine duty: you *shall* love your neighbor as yourself.

We obey the Great Commandment by adoration and obedience. We strive to obey and be like him whom we adore, and that means works of love.

Source of all love, let me never forget that you loved me first. Let me never forget that you are in the middle of every one of my relationships, that it is not a relationship of me—neighbor, but me—God—neighbor. Amen

LOVING THE UNLOVELY, THE UNLOVABLE

"Just as 'faith' is a dialectical qualification, so also is true Christian love. Therefore Christianity teaches specifically that one ought to love his enemy, that the pagan, too, loves his friend. . . .When a person loves his friend, it is by no means clear that he loves God, but when a person loves his enemy, it is clear that he fears and loves God, and only in this way can God be loved" (Kierkegaard 1967).

hom does one as a rule choose as a friend? With whom does one as a rule fall in love? Whom does one choose to marry? Someone who is lovable, of course! Someone whom one's instinctive, inclinational, spontaneous love is able to love. It is easy, so easy, to love a lovely lovable person—until one falls out of love, until the two become incompatible and quarrel, until the object of one's instinctive, inclinational, spontaneous love becomes unlovable—indeed, becomes hateable! Suddenly the very same instinctive, inclinational, spontaneous feeling changes, and one becomes able to hate and is unable to love.

But it seems that the second of Christ's great commandments asks us to love the ugly, the unlovely, the unlovable! That must mean those human beings who are blemishes and blots on the humanscape: That nasty neighbor who chases the neighborhood kids if they step on his lawn to retrieve a ball. That bully kid who terrorizes the children on the way home from school. That wife who has turned into a nag and a crab. That lovable child who has suddenly been transformed into a vulgar, boorish, ungrateful teenager.

So I am supposed to love those people whom I find unacceptable. Sorry, I find that unacceptable! My whole nature cries, "No thanks! I have no inclination to love the ugly, to say nothing of loving my enemies!"

God, you ask me to love the ugly. You ask me to love my enemies. God, I am not able! I am unable! I can't do it! Help! I need the help of your Holy Spirit! Amen

BACK TO NEED AGAIN!

"What does it mean to be a Christian? It means to walk under the eye of the Heavenly Father, therefore under the eye of the truly loving Father, led by Christ's hand, and strengthened by the witness of the Holy Spirit. O, blessed companionship" (Kierkegaard 1967).

ove the unlovely? Love the ugly? Do not ask yourself if you are able to do it, says Kierkegaard, for then you will not be able. No, ready or not, able or not, you and I must be obedient to Christ's two great commandments—and then the Spirit, "the only vitalizing, enabling power for the future" comes to our assistance. Here we come back to need again! "To need God is man's highest perfection." You and I desperately need the Holy Spirit in his double role of Comforter and Strengthener.

In gratitude to God for the gift of his boundless grace in Christ Jesus and full of holy resolve to begin the completely new life we have through him, we venture to begin. But in a very short time we discover that the very best we can do is shabby and imperfect. We are unable to do it! Then and only then do we call upon the Holy Enabler! Only when we begin trying to make the possibility of the new life in Christ into actuality do we come into the situation of need that makes us cry out: Help! Help! I am weak and powerless! Holy Spirit, be my power and my strength as well as my comforter in my weakness.

"We human beings carry the holy only in fragile jars, but You, O Holy Spirit, when You live in a person You live in what is infinitely inferior: You Spirit of Holiness, You live in our filth and impurity, You Spirit of Wisdom, you live in our foolishness, You Spirit of Truth, you live in our self-deception! O, stay here, and You, who do not conveniently look for a desirable residence, which You would seek in vain, You, who creating and giving new birth, make your new dwelling place, O, stay here that it may at some time come to be that you are delighted with the house You yourself prepared for yourself in my filthy and foolish and cheating heart. Amen" (Kierkegaard 1967).

O. HALLESBY

Carroll and Mary Hinderlie

WESTERN CIVILIZATION IS SHAPED BY ACTS 9:11: "BEHOLD, HE IS praying!" We are the prayer children of the apostle Paul who declared, "In Christ's name I declare to you the forgiveness of sins!" In prayer is born our continual energy of youthful renewal.

Small wonder then that in World War II Franklin D. Roosevelt, the man who led America through that crisis, kept a copy of *Prayer* by O. Hallesby nearby. The paperback and the hardback both belonged at his bedside with his initials on them.

Hallesby's theme that prayer is "helplessness, simply opening the door to Jesus!" may have led to the incident in which a comment was made that FDR had a simple faith. But simple faith is not simplistic. There is nothing simplistic in Hallesby's treatment of the topic of prayer.

Hallesby was one of Norway's most popular authors of devotional books. Studying under him in 1939–40 at the independent seminary in Oslo, we found also that he was one of its most beloved professors.

As a teacher, Hallesby loved dialogue. His classrooms were socratic, always beginning with "Herr _____, can you tell me . . . ?" His chuckle captured us with its familiarity. Classes began with the half hour he had spent with us on our knees before each lecture. He practiced what he prayed so that we felt we had a modern Hans Nielsen Hauge in his "transparency." Like Hauge, he remained a layman, refusing to be ordained.

WHAT PRAYER IS

"To pray is to let Jesus come into our hearts. This teaches us, in the first place, that it is not our prayer which moves the Lord Jesus. It is Jesus who moves us to pray. He knocks. Thereby He makes known His desire to come in to us. Our prayers are always a result of Jesus' knocking at our hearts' doors. This throws new light upon the old prophetic message: 'Before they call, I will answer; and while they are yet speaking, I will hear' (Isa. 65:24)" (Hallesby 1931).

Prayer is response to God's seeking. Usually we think of prayer as initiated by us. We are the ones who are generating the power to pray. It is not so. We pray first because we are lost—and found, dead—become alive, and all because of the four letter word *help*.

Most people who remember Edvard Munch's famous painting "The Scream" would not see it as an illustration of prayer. I don't know that Dr. Hallesby would. But for one to whom the Spirit has revealed the thoughts of the soul, the cry for help can indeed be such a scream. To sense something of what it means to live before God helps us to understand our lostness, our deadness. Our cry for help is the beginning of a life of prayer, of response to the searching passionate love of God.

The psalmist says it for us: "Thou hast said, 'Seek ye my face.' My heart says to thee, 'Thy face, LORD, I do seek'" (Ps. 27:8). This is the pulse of the heart in prayer. Only God can produce this longing for himself; only God can satisfy.

Prayer is a life lived in God's expectancy of our lives. The calling to be *you,* the calling to be *me,* is a lifetime of renewal in prayer as God calls forth the new in each of us every morning. Return and renewal happens daily. Daily we "crawl back to our baptism," Luther tells us, as we share his body and blood in Holy Communion. He renews our life of prayer and fellowship with him.

And not to us only, O Lord, but to all who love thy appearing. Amen

PRAYER AND FAITH

"When an honest soul examines himself in the light of the Scriptures, he soon finds that faith is just what seems to be lacking in his prayers. It says that he should ask in faith, nothing doubting. He does just the opposite. . . . 'a double minded man, unstable in all his ways.' He is in distress, helpless; and he prays" (Hallesby 1931).

Hallesby reminds us of the many times that Jesus says, "Your faith has saved you." And what did that faith look like? It was simply coming to Jesus and "pleading their distress before Him, whether it was physical or spiritual or both." It is given a clear image for our doubting hearts in those words that have echoed this cry of all of us in our tunnel of despair, "I do believe; help thou my unbelief!"

It is the paradox of our lives—believing and doubting. But only when we come to Jesus in our helplessness and hear His radical answer, "If thou canst! All things are possible to him that believeth"—only then do we give way and confess that Jesus must also create faith in us.

It is essential for us that we go to the words of Jesus to get the firsthand information about prayer and faith. Out of this springs all the wealth of Acts and the Epistles that are constant resources and strength for our lives in prayer. When we keep ourselves in the words of our Lord and the words of the apostles, we understand that the energy for the life of prayer comes from the love of the Savior. This energy produces a life of companionship in prayer.

Lord, we want to live in your love. Your love for us promises a life of prayer like yours, because it is yours alone to give. We cannot make it on our own. We can listen to your promises in Paul's letter to the Philippians: "Have no anxiety about anything, but in everything by prayer and supplication with thanksgiving let your requests be made known to God" (Phil. 4:6). Amen

DIFFICULTIES IN PRAYER

"To pray, really to pray, is what is difficult for us. It feels like too much of an effort. . . . Prayer can become a burden for us. . . . The more of an effort prayer becomes, the more easily it is neglected. . . .We feel more and more alienated from God, and therefore less and less eager to speak with Him. Then we develop an unwilling spirit which always finds pretexts for not praying and excuses for having neglected prayer" (Hallesby 1931).

 ometimes our very helplessness freezes us into inaction and despair. "Our words fly up, our thoughts remain below." Often a good hymn can rescue us from that numbness.

Our life in a Japanese prison camp during World War II would have been bleak indeed if we had not had the treasure house of hymns that we had memorized as children and as young Christians. A month after we missionaries were imprisoned, I was sent into a hospital away from camp, away from our new baby, away from all who were dear to me. I was not alone. Jesus spoke clearly and personally through those hymns, some of them centuries old . . . some were psalms from before Jesus' time on earth. They sang joy and a sturdy comfort into my frightened soul. They literally shouted at me as I looked out of the hospital ward with the window that opened only to a wall that would sometimes reflect a ray of sunlight.

It was the ringing chorus from Romans 14:8 "Whether we live therefore, or die, we are the Lord's" in the Epiphany hymn, "We Are the Lord's" that became my bulwark:

> *We are the Lord's: His all sufficient merit,*
> *Sealed on the cross to us this grace accords;*
> *We are the Lord's, and all things shall inherit;*
> *Whether we live or die, we are the Lord's.*
> —*The Lutheran Hymnary,* Augsburg

Prayer strength returned in prison camp over and over again with the witness of the hymns and the psalms—the prayers of God's pilgrim people with whom we were privileged to be fellow travelers! Blessed be God. Amen

READ AS SLOWLY AS YOU CAN

"As you kneel to speak with your Lord, it seems as though everything you have to do appears vividly before your mind's eye. You see especially how much there is to do, and how urgent it is that it be done. As these thoughts occur, you become more and more restless. You try to keep your thoughts collected and to speak with God, but you succeed only for a moment now and then. The time on your knees is just that much time wasted. Then you stop praying" (Hallesby 1931).

It was Roland Bainton who suggested the motto for the Meditation Library at the retreat center, Holden Village. The motto is "Read as slowly as you can." The sin of impatience breaks down our communication lines with one another, with ourselves, and certainly with the Scriptures and with God in prayer.

"As slowly as you can." Think about this when you take time for prayer. We decide to take a specific hour in our day, or part of it, for prayer. What happens? Hallesby had experienced this and described it well.

How can we recapture our prayer post? We need to learn to let every thought be captive to Christ. In Philippians Paul has this strong conclusion to his advice on the attitude of prayer. Hallesby reminds us of this verse: "And the peace of God, which passes all understanding, will keep your hearts and your minds in Christ Jesus" (Phil. 4:7).

When we read Scripture as an entrance to prayer, communication begins again. It was the medieval bishop, Anselm, reading Scripture meant absorbing a text until it became a prayer. This meant for Anselm that prayer was simple in style for all believers, but "costing not less than everything."

Prayer happens when we know inwardly as well as objectively that we are helpless, needing God: "Come now, little man, turn aside for awhile from your daily employment, escape for a moment from the tumult of your thoughts. Put aside your weighty cares, let your burdensome distractions wait, free yourself awhile for God and rest awhile in him" (Anselm 1973).

Jesus says, "Come away . . . and rest awhile." Even so, Lord Jesus. Amen

PRAYING IN THE NAME OF JESUS

"To pray in the name of Jesus is, in all likelihood, the deepest mystery in prayer. It is therefore exceedingly difficult for the Spirit of prayer to explain this to us. Furthermore, it is easier for us to forget this than anything else which the Spirit teaches us.

"The name of Jesus is the greatest mystery in heaven and on earth. In heaven, this mystery is known; on earth it is unknown to most people. No one can fathom it fully.

"The longer a sinner stands in the heavenly light which the Spirit of God has shed upon him . . . the more he feels that God cannot have anything to do with anyone who is as impure and dishonest as he is.

"To him the Spirit of prayer says, 'Come, in the name of Jesus.' That name gives unholy men access to a holy God" (Hallesby 1931).

Prayer in the name of Jesus is to pray in the strength and power of that name. In our business world, naming a name often gives entrance; it gives a recommendation. The power lies in the name, not in the person who repeats it. In a far more profound way, to pray, to enter in prayer in the name of Jesus is to come into a kingdom of a different nature, so different as to be frightening, certainly awe inspiring if we dared to take time to meditate on it. How can we approach God, the Promiser who never fails, with our lives strewn with fragments of broken promises crowding our memories? How can we expect to pray when we are such strangers to that kingdom of love and mercy and so ego-centered even in our prayers? Do we dare link ourselves with the Name of Jesus in the solitude of prayer?

We not only dare to pray in the Name; we are commanded to do so. That name embodies for us the grace to come in prayer, "to pour out our hearts like water" before God, thanking God that we know this grace. We know the love of God in the name of Jesus that overcomes all our fear, even the fear of not being heard.

Blessed be God! Amen

THE IMAGE OF GOD AND THE REALITY OF PRAYER

"What we do in God's kingdom is entirely dependent upon what we are. And what we are depends again upon what we receive. And what we receive, depends again upon prayer. This applies not only to the work of God in us, but the work of God through us. . . . Every believer presents a daily influx into this world of eternity's powers of salvation . . . and helps to transform this world into God's kingdom. These believing prayers are unquestionably the means by which God, in the quickest way, would be able to give to the world these saving powers from the realm of eternity which are necessary before Christ's return" (Hallesby 1931).

Hallesby asks the question we ask: "Are our intercessions really necessary?" The answer is clear. Jesus says that it is God who must send forth the workers for the harvest, but also that he is dependent upon our prayer. It is impossible for God to bring the world forward to its goal without human beings. God has voluntarily bound himself to us in his governance of the world.

103

An image from the late Herbert Butterfield, an English philosopher of history, reinforces the words of Hallesby. Butterfield sees history as a great orchestration with all of us involved. Like Hallesby, Butterfield sees God as the symphony conductor, composing as he directs according to the way that each of us plays or does not play her or his part.

This image of God being dependent upon our prayers is like the question Kierkegaard asked, "How could an Almighty God create beings who were independent of their Creator?" Kierkegaard concludes, as we must, with another question, the final one, "Who else?"

"I appeal to you, brethren, by our Lord Jesus Christ and by the love of the Spirit, to strive together with me in your prayers to God on my behalf . . ." (Rom. 15:30).

PRAYER AS WORK

"Christians of our day are busy people. We do not live for nothing in the cen-tury of work. Never in the history of God's church have His people worked more than now. And never have we had so many workers . . . or been so well organized as it is today" (Hallesby 1931).

But in all this machinery of activity, there is one job that cannot be done by computers or machines. The job is to pray. The actual work of praying has to be done by indi-vidual people; there is no shortcut, no substitute.

We look on prayer as our daily breath. We do get outside our own little group and pray for larger needs occasionally. Still, the eas-iest way is to stay in the old patterns. We are not energetic enough to venture out into the fields of God where the harvest waits.

The Spirit of prayer will lead us, if we ask. We hear our Lord saying, "Go ye into all the world . . ." When did you put up a map of the world where you and your household could see it daily and be reminded that our beloved John 3:16 means just that: the world is peopled with human beings whom Jesus came to save. We so quickly adjust ourselves to the fact that there are so many needs, so many places and frightening situations, so much suffering and what are we, a small family group among so much? "And the disciples said to him, 'Where are we to get bread enough in the desert to feed so great a crowd?' And Jesus said to them, 'How many loaves have you?' They said, 'Seven, and a few small fish'" (Matt. 15:33–34). That is the word for us. All we need to do is remember to whom we belong and re-read the Gospels and the Acts of the Apostles, and ask the Spirit of prayer to enlighten our imaginations to pray around this great planet, beloved and redeemed by its creator.

Now enter that "closet" that Kierkegaard said held the lever that could move the world, prayer! "Call to me and I will answer you, and will tell you great and hidden things which you have not known" (Jer. 33:3).

We believe you, O Lord, help our unbelief. Amen

PRAYER IS FOR GLORIFYING GOD

"Prayer is ordained for the purpose of glorifying the name of God. If we will make use of prayer, not to wrest from God advantages for ourselves or our dear ones, or to escape from tribulations and difficulties, but to call down upon ourselves and others those things which will glorify the name of God . . . then we shall see such answers to prayer as we had never thought were possible" (Hallesby 1931).

One woman I knew closed prayer with the phrase "And, God, we will give you all the glory." It sounded almost phoney to me, but I knew the person who was praying— she was real. It makes it sound as if God were greedily on the lookout as to who gets the credit. How totally anthropomorphic we are in our conception of such a phrase as "the glory of God." How could we possibly understand even a slight bit of it, except as we catch a glimpse of it in our Lord Jesus? And when he referred to the glory of God it had something to do with making people whole. To make people whole is to glorify God; to glorify God is to make people whole.

When this conviction takes root in us, we come to the Lord with a deep sense of need, asking for the true Spirit of prayer. And as our Lord prays with us and through us, the glory of God will be borne out in the lives of those for whom we pray. From icy mountains to tropical deserts, jungles of forests to jungles of asphalt, continents apart—but no farther apart in reality than each of us is from the grace of God. That is the geography of prayer. The planet shall be made whole to the glory of God in Christ Jesus.

Thine be the glory, forever. Amen

PRAYER IN THE CROSS

Prayer is always centered in the cross. It is one activity of the disciple that allows for no ego satisfaction. It is not like the feeling one has while sharing a profound insight for the mutual benefit of the Bible class, or challenging and inspiring groups for greater sacrifice or more specific commitments. Even when one confesses one's own faults and sins, there creeps in the shadow of the ego again, even if one has suffered in the telling.

So, what is it with prayer that makes it unique in the life of the Christian? First, it is a solitary task, at least much of the time. We do not grow in intimate prayer life with our Lord if we are always in public. And the very solitude of the prayer time is an anxiety and at times becomes a burden. It is lifetime growth. Just as our lives have ups and downs, so does our prayer life.

Then it is difficult to let go and let Jesus speak out of the word or out of silence. But sometimes situations and people to be prayed for come into one's line of vision. In the solitude of prayer, in our very anxious and weak spirits, God speaks, and in that speech there is the energy-giving power to do, to be, to act.

Hallesby suggests that this lifetime school of prayer was never promised as a crash course. There is something about this school of prayer which tries our patience sorely. Jesus himself alludes to it on several occasions, especially in Luke 18:1–8, where he says "that they ought always to pray and not lose heart."

Hallesby also says, *"We become faint very easily. How many times have we not earnestly resolved in our own minds to pray for certain people and for certain causes, only to find ourselves growing faint? We were not willing to expend the effort. And little by little we ceased to intercede for others"* (1931).

Prayer can never be a source of pride, so seldom do we see results. When we do see results we can never point to them as ours! So we live our prayer life, as all of our life, under the cross, putting all our faint-hearted efforts there where he "who writes straight with crooked lines" can also use us to further the kingdom.

Thy kingdom come, Thy will be done. Amen

GOSPEL AND LAW IN PRAYER

"My one desire has been to preach the gospel of prayer without setting aside the laws governing prayer life" (Hallesby 1931).

To be before God without forgiveness is an impossible life. That is the entrance to prayer. Without prayer's access to God our lives would wither up in unbelief, despair, and eternal fear.

Hallesby's *Prayer* is most clear on the order of the life of prayer. It is not a series of steps that we master. The priority is our helplessness, our need which Jesus not only creates, but satisfies when we open the door to his knock. The climate of the book is grace, grace, grace as the ongoing sustenance of the prayer life.

The difficulties of prayer life, its problems, wrestlings, misuse, meaning, and varying styles of expression are all here. They are all, however, in the context of the one source and reason for this life, Jesus Christ, who never promised us a "rose garden." But he did promise us himself, and that makes all the difference.

Jesus is not only the "end" of the communication, Jesus is also the "means." The daily interweaving of our lives with his makes our prayer lives grow, even when we are unaware of it. The problem with writing about prayer is that because we are individuals we should not take the pattern of prayer from anyone else. We have to remember the one prayer our Lord taught the disciples, and let him teach each one of us from there.

The life of discipleship, the life of prayer—can they be separated? How well Jesus knows us! He is continually reminding the first disciples and the latest ones to "watch and pray," and that "the spirit is willing but the flesh is weak." Only the Lord can tighten the muscles, sharpen the vision, pour compassion into hearts of stone to motivate the life of the Christian to perseverance in prayer. When the great Hallelujahs are re-echoing through the universes, perhaps then we shall know that prayer is just beginning!

Come quickly, Lord Jesus. Amen.

DIETRICH BONHOEFFER

Hubert Nelson

IT WAS IN THE EARLY, GRAY DAWN OF APRIL 9, 1945, THAT German theologian and pastor Dietrich Bonhoeffer was executed in the concentration camp at Flossenburg by special order of Heinrich Himmler. The charge against him was treason for his part in the attempted assassination of Adolf Hitler on July 20, 1944. For Bonhoeffer, his resistance to Nazism was an act of obedience to Jesus Christ.

"For innumerable Christians in Germany, on the Continent, in England, and in America, Dietrich Bonhoeffer's death has been a contemporary affirmation of Tertullian's dictum: the blood of the martyrs is the seed of the church; for his life and death and his writings throb with the simple, downright faith of one who has met Jesus Christ and accepted the ultimate consequences of that encounter in the world" (Bonhoeffer 1954).

Bonhoeffer was 16 when he chose to study theology and by the age of 21 he presented his doctor's thesis. In 1928-29 he was assistant pastor of a German-speaking congregation in Barcelona. The following year he was an exchange student at Union Theological Seminary in New York City, and returned in 1931 to teach systematic theology at the University of Berlin. Bonhoeffer came from a privileged background. The future was his. He was willing to sacrifice all of that for a higher call.

In 1933 Hitler and the National Socialist Party came to power. Young Bonhoeffer recognized that there was a subtle shift from respecting the office to worshiping the leader who held the office. He recognized and resisted the growing anti-Semitism. In 1935 he was appointed by the Confessing Church to organize and head an illegal, clandestine seminary in Finkenwald for the training of pastors in Pomerania. By 1938 Bonhoeffer was forbidden to teach or write or publish and was identified as an enemy of Nazi Germany. Although he had an opportunity to escape his impending fate in 1939 while in the United States, he felt compelled to return and be a part of the struggle of his people. His part in the resistance movement, which sought the life of the evil dictator, resulted in his execution only weeks before the arrival of the Allies.

In the following selections from several of Bonhoeffer's books, a common motif is grace, which Bonhoeffer saw as the interpretive center of all of life. But, as we will see, grace was always both promise and demand, gift and response, free and costly, gospel and law.

GRACE AND OLD TESTAMENT

"It is only when one knows the unutterability of the name of God that one can utter the name of Jesus Christ; it is only when one loves life and earth so much that without them everything seems to be over that one can believe in the resurrection and a new world; it is only when one submits to God's law that one can speak of grace; and it is only when God's wrath and vengeance are hanging as grim realities over the heads of one's enemies that something of what it means to love and forgive them can touch our hearts. In my opinion it is not Christian to want to take our thoughts and feelings too quickly and too directly from the New Testament" (Bonhoeffer 1965b).

It was not until I was 17 years old that I began to see my life in context. I worked as an orderly in a nursing home. There was time for many conversations. Mostly, I just listed to stories that happened long before I was born. One man was a railroad contractor who helped build railroads into the western frontiers. One had been a farmer who cleared a piece of virgin land in southwestern Minnesota. One had been a grocer, another an attorney. Some had families and some were all alone in their autumn years. But, that year, listening to their stories gave me a context in which to look at my life. A context for my dreams, my values, my youth, my successes, my failures, my schooling, and my occupation.

The Old Testament in some sense provides a context in which to understand the riches of grace in the New Testament. For two millennia the people of God had experienced God's gracious acts. The call of Abraham, the Exodus, the mercies shown to David, the promises of Isaiah to the exiles, to name only a few.

But there is also an earthiness and a frankness with which the story of the Old Testament is told that places the New Testament in the context of the real world. The Old Testament helps us understand the importance of the humanity of our Savior. It provides a context for the receiving of the Christ.

"In many and various ways God spoke of old to our fathers by the prophets; but in these last days he has spoken to us by a Son" (Heb. 1:1–2).

GRACE AND COMMUNITY

"Christian [community] is not an ideal, but a divine reality. . . . Innumerable times a whole Christian community has broken down because it had sprung from a wish dream. The serious Christian, set down for the first time in a Christian community, is likely to bring with [one] a very definite idea of what Christian life together should be and try to realize it. But God's grace speedily shatters such dreams. Just as surely as God desires to lead us to a knowledge of genuine Christian fellowship, so surely must we be overwhelmed by a great disillusionment with others, with ourselves. . . .

"Only that fellowship which faces such disillusionment, with all its unhappy and ugly aspects, begins to be what it should be in God's sight, begins to grasp in faith the promise that is given to it. . . . [The person] who loves [one's] dream of a community more than the Christian community itself becomes a destroyer of the latter, even though [one's] personal intentions may be ever so honest and earnest and sacrificial" (Bonhoeffer 1954).

 often ask new members why they chose to join our congregation. It is easy to be lifted to great heights by their responses. "This is such a warm and friendly congregation. The preaching gives me something to take home each week. There isn't all that talk about money often heard in other churches. . . ." I usually bask in the warmth of such comments but later think to myself, "Will they want to remain when they find out what we really are like?"

Every member of every congregation is bound to be shocked or disillusioned sooner or later when they discover not only the humanity but utter sinfulness of fellow members. Those who are able to stay in a congregation and commit themselves to its fellowship are those who have discovered that it is God who has brought them together and it is by God's grace that they are a community.

"Now as they were eating, Jesus took bread, and blessed, and broke it, and gave it to the disciples and said, 'Take, eat; this is my body.' And he took a cup, and when he had given thanks he gave it to them, saying, 'Drink of it, all of you; for this is my blood of the covenant, which is poured out for many for the forgiveness of sins"(Matt. 26:26–28).

GRACE AND LAW I

"It is grace to know God's commands. They release us from self-made plans and conflicts. They make our steps certain and our way joyful. God gives his commands in order that we may fulfill them, and 'his commandments are not burdensome' (1 John 5:3) for [the one] who has found all salvation in Jesus Christ. Jesus has himself been under the law and has fulfilled it in total obedience to the Father. God's will becomes [one's] joy, his nourishment. So he gives thanks in us for the grace of the law and grants to us joy in its fulfillment" (Bonhoeffer 1970).

The prophet Amos once spoke of a famine that was worse than any famine of food (Amos 8:11). It was a famine of the word of God. Nothing could be more devastating than to seek a word from God and to be met only by silence.

Quentin, in Miller's play, "After the Fall," had a dream in which he stood before the bench to plead his case and the bench was empty. Even a word of judgment would have been better than no word at all. The most devastating judgment of all is no word, that it just doesn't matter one way or another. Despair is to discover that there is no other person or standard by which one's life is being evaluated.

113

It is an experience of grace, therefore, to discover that God cares enough to share his Word with us. What joy could be greater than to realize that the creator of this universe is so interested in you and me that he actually discloses his will and purposes to us. You and I make a difference to God. The way we live our lives makes a difference to him. No wonder that we say that the greatest expression of grace was the Word of God become flesh. So we too join with the psalmist and Bonhoeffer and give thanks for the grace of law.

"I am a sojourner on earth; hide not thy commandments from me! My soul is consumed with longing for thy ordinances at all times"(Ps. 119:19–20).

GRACE AND LAW II

"No one understands the law of God who does not know about the deliverance which has happened and the promise of what is to come. The one who asks about the law is reminded about Jesus Christ and the deliverance of human beings from the bondage of sin and death which has been completed in him, reminded of the new beginnings which God has made for all people in Jesus Christ. . . .

"God's law cannot be separated from his act of deliverance. The God of the ten commandments is the God who led you out of the land of Egypt (Ex. 20:2). God gives his law to those whom he loves, those whom he has chosen and taken to himself (Deut. 7:7–11). To know God's law is grace and joy (Deut. 4:6–10). It is the way of life for those who accept God's grace (Lev. 18:5)" (Bonhoeffer 1986).

114

Ehme Osterbur, former Lutheran bishop, once shared that the law, no matter how tough or firmly spoken, never expressed anything but love when spoken by his mother. The same command expressed much more tamely and softly spoken would often make him bristle when spoken by someone else.

What was the difference? The difference was the context. When his mother spoke it was always in the context of love. Love that had proved itself again and again and again. He knew without reservation that his mother was for him, on his side. His mother had literally given herself, often at great sacrifice, that he might know joy and beauty and happiness.

God's law, when spoken by some, makes us bristle. For the context is not love. God's law must always be received in the context of God's love. It is the one who has delivered us, whose mercy is without limit, who was willing to give up the glories of heaven and even die for us, who also gives us his commands. In that context we see God's law as an expression of God's grace.

"This is my commandment . . . you are my friends . . ."(John 15:12, 14).

GRACE AND OBEDIENCE

"'Only [one] who believes is obedient, and only [one] who is obedient believes.' It is quite unbiblical to hold the first proposition without the second. . . . For faith is only real when there is obedience, never without it, and faith only becomes faith in the act of obedience. . . . If we are to believe, we must obey a concrete command. Without this preliminary step of obedience, our faith will only be pious humbug, and lead us to grace which is not costly. Everything depends on the first step. It has a unique quality of its own. The first step of obedience makes Peter leave his nets, and later get out of the ship; it calls upon the young man to leave his riches. Only this new existence, created through obedience, can make faith possible" (Bonhoeffer 1966).

 s it possible to believe in Jesus Christ and trust him and yet be disobedient? If this were not true, then who of us could be called believers? And yet, if God's grace is received but does not change us in any way, then God has not really been able to give us anything.

Suppose that we were traveling by night in the land of the enemy. We have been told that we will be coming to a critical intersection shortly before dawn. At that intersection will be a woman. She has chosen to risk her own life so that she might direct travelers down the path that leads to life and safety.

When we arrive at the intersection, it is as we have been told. We meet the woman and she points to a fairly narrow path. The other roads look to be more traveled. The road pointed to even appears to be going in the wrong direction. What do you do first? Do you decide whether or not to believe her, or whether or not to obey her? It would seem to be a moot point, for in that concrete situation, the two would seem to be the same. If you obey her you believe her, and if you believe her you obey her. In the concrete situations of life, faith and obedience cannot be separated.

"But someone will say, 'You have faith and I have works.' Show me your faith apart from your works, and I by my works will show you my faith"(James 2:18).

GRACE AND DISCIPLESHIP

"We Lutherans have gathered . . . round the carcass of cheap grace, and there we have drunk of the poison which has killed the life of following Christ. . . . We gave away the word and sacrament wholesale, we baptized, confirmed, and absolved a whole nation without asking awkward questions or insisting on strict conditions. Our humanitarian sentiment made us give that which was holy to the scornful and unbelieving.We poured forth unending streams of grace. But the call to follow Jesus in the narrow way was hardly ever heard. . . .What had happened to all those warnings of Luther's against preaching the gospel in such a manner as to make [people] rest secure in their ungodly living?" (Bonhoeffer 1966).

 remember a teacher coming into our classroom after lunch, tears rolling down her cheeks. "What's the matter?" someone asked. "A former student told me that he never learned a thing in my class, that I was the worst teacher he had ever had."

The class was suddenly silent. We loved her but we also knew that the former student was probably right. She did whatever we wanted. Homework could be forgiven. She would go over our tests with us, allowing us to change the answers and improve our grades. She liked us, but not enough to take the risk of disciplining us and demanding commitment to our studies.

Bonhoeffer felt that the church in his day dispensed grace much like that teacher dispensed education. It was benevolently doled out in generous quantities to whomever put their hands out, but it was essentially worthless. It could not resist the forces of evil, whether it be the Nazi party or in any other shape or form.

It is impossible to receive the full richness of God's grace apart from the costliness of discipleship. Grace and the discipline of Jesus Christ cannot be separated.

"And he called to him the multitude with his disciples, and said to them, 'If any man would come after me, let him deny himself and take up his cross and follow me. For whoever would save his life will lose it; and whoever loses his life for my sake and the gospel's will save it'"(Mark 8:34—35).

GRACE AND SUFFERING

O Lord God, great distress has come upon me;
my cares threaten to crush me, and I do not know what to do.
O God, be gracious to me and help me.
Give me strength to bear what thou dost send,
and do not let fear rule over me;
Take a father's care of my wife and children.
O merciful God, forgive me all the sins that I have committed
against thee and against [other people].
I trust in thy grace and commit my life wholly into thy hands.
Do with me according to thy will and as is best for me.
Whether I live or die, I am with thee, and thou, my God, art with me.
Lord, I wait for thy salvation and for thy kingdom. Amen
(Bonhoeffer 1965b)

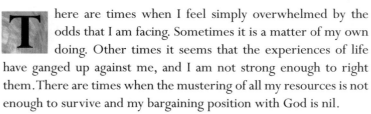

There are times when I feel simply overwhelmed by the odds that I am facing. Sometimes it is a matter of my own doing. Other times it seems that the experiences of life have ganged up against me, and I am not strong enough to right them. There are times when the mustering of all my resources is not enough to survive and my bargaining position with God is nil.

It is at those moments that God's grace in Jesus Christ is like a light shining in the darkness. To be able to let go and let God take over is literally our salvation. To trust that our Lord can meet all the odds gives a peace beyond understanding.

Bonhoeffer made it very clear that it is not our job to create these gaps for God to fill. We need not try to make people feel lousy so that God can make them feel good. Jesus Christ comes to us at the very center of our existence in both good times and bad. His love creates also our need for his love. But never is God's grace more beautiful than when we are simply overwhelmed by the odds that we are facing.

"Father, if thou art willing, remove this cup from me; nevertheless not my will, but thine, be done" (Luke 22:42).

GRACE AND GOD'S WILL

"The will of God is not a system of rules which is established from the outset; it is something new and different in each different situation in life, and for this reason a [person] must ever anew examine what the will of God may be. . . . Our knowledge of God's will is not something over which we ourselves dispose, but it depends solely upon the grace of God, and this grace is and requires to be new every morning. The voice of the heart is not to be confused with the will of God, nor is any kind of inspiration or any general principle, for the will of God discloses itself ever anew only to [the one] who proves it ever anew. . . .

"For this reason there arises every day anew the question how here, today and in my present situation I am to remain and to be preserved in this new life with God, with Jesus Christ. And this is just the question which is involved in proving what is the will of God" (Bonhoeffer, *Ethics*, 1965a).

For more than half of my years as a pastor I served as copastor with one of my best friends. Most people said that such a relationship would be impossible. Others asked for documentation and procedural policies that defined how we made it work. Basically our copastor style worked well for thirteen years for two reasons. First, we had a deep and real friendship, and second, we agreed that the mission of the church was to take precedence over our personal or professional ambitions. Both of these had to be worked at and nurtured, but they were a reality. It was a style of pastoring that we lived out in freedom day by day.

This is a kind of homely illustration of the way that you and I seek to live within the will of God. There is freedom granted to us but it is not chaotic or lawless.

We seek to know God's will in the context of two realities. We have been given the gift of God's deep and never ending friendship in Jesus Christ. And, second, we have been called through our Baptism to share the cross of our Lord. Thus, it is grace that defines even something so important as seeking God's will.

"Beloved, if God so loved us, we also ought to love one another" (1 John 4:11).

GRACE AND WORRIES

"Please don't ever get anxious or worried about me, but don't forget to pray for me—I'm sure you don't! I am so sure of God's guiding hand that I hope I shall always be kept in that certainty. You must never doubt that I am traveling with gratitude and cheerfulness along the road where I am being led. My past life is brimful of God's goodness, and my sins are covered by the forgiving love of Christ crucified. I am most thankful for the people I have met, and I only hope that they never have to grieve about me, but that they, too, will always be certain of, and thankful for, God's mercy and forgiveness. Forgive me for writing this" (Bonhoeffer 1965b).

I never seem to worry when I look back. As with Bonhoeffer, I see an orderly pattern to my former journeys. I recognize God's guiding hand and the many ways my life has been touched by his love and protected by his providence. And when I recall my failures and even willful disobedience, I recall how God's forgiveness covered them all. Looking back over my shoulder seldom activates any real worries.

Worries come when I look ahead. Especially when I look ahead beyond the shadow of my remembrance of God's past grace. It is at these moments that I need others to pray for me and minister to me. When my memory becomes too short to give me confidence for the future, it is the longer and clearer memory of others that assures me of the sufficiency of God's grace.

Bonhoeffer tried to share his worries in such a way that they would not ignite further the worries of his friends and family. He tried to be their priest assuring them of God's grace while at the same time asking that they would be his priest. We need each other if grace is to truly dispel our worries.

"I can do all things in him who strengthens me. Yet it was kind of you to share my trouble"(Phil. 4:13–14).

GRACE AND MEALTIME

"God must feed us. We cannot and dare not demand this food as our right, for we, poor sinners, have not merited it. Thus the sustenance that God provides becomes a consolation of the afflicted; for it is the token of the grace and faithfulness with which God supports and guides His children. True, the Scriptures say, 'If any will not work, neither let him eat' (2 Thess. 3:10), and thus make the receiving of bread strictly dependent upon working for it. But the Scriptures do not say anything about any claim that the working person has upon God for his bread. The work is commanded, indeed, but the bread is God's free and gracious gift. We cannot simply take it for granted that our work provides us with bread; this is rather God's order of grace" (Bonhoeffer 1954).

There is a sense in which we always come to our tables as a people who have come from the Lord's Table. We have been asked to be a people who eat in remembrance. We remember our hunger, and we remember the unmerited gift of God that satisfied and continues to satisfy that hunger.

When we come to our tables we are invited to remember not only God but all the people who, on behalf of God, have served us that our hunger might be satisfied. The ones who planted and cultivated, the ones who fed and cared for the livestock and poultry or caught the fish, those who harvested and prepared food for consumption, the ones who distributed and marketed those things that fill our cupboards and refrigerators, and then the ones at home or in restaurants who cook and serve. We experience a continuation of the grace experienced at the Lord's Table at our own tables.

Finally we remember those who are calling us to share and to serve that they might receive the same table grace that we have enjoyed. And, when we have learned to give and to share with those whose stomachs are empty, we experience grace again. We have been allowed to feed our Lord at our table even as he has fed us at his table.

"For I was hungry and you gave me food"(Matt. 25:35).

SIMONE WEIL

Jeanette Strandjord

THERE ARE MANY WAYS TO DESCRIBE SIMONE WEIL (1909–1943). T. S. Eliot speaks of her as a great soul, a saint. Many would add that they see her as a genius, one who wrestled with and wrote profoundly about issues of truth and justice. She is also seen as a person of great integrity. She not only wrote, but lived, what she believed. She brought this same commitment to Jesus Christ after her conversion in 1938.

Finally, though her work is of great depth and seriousness, it is also penetrated by warmth, humor, and great passion. This saint, serious and blessed with genius, loved God, her neighbor, and the world.

In 1928 Weil began her studies at what was regarded the finest school in France. There her brilliance was recognized and she completed her degree in philosophy at the age of twenty-two. She then turned her attention to teaching. She enjoyed this as well as being involved in local political concerns.

Weil's political interests led her into activities on behalf of local unemployed workers. In deep sympathy with their situation, she took leave of teaching and went to work at a car factory. This was not the last time Weil would voluntarily shed her position and comfort to join in the work and suffering of others. Later she would travel to Spain during its civil war, not to fight, but to support the anti-fascist forces. Then, after her faith conversion, she would take a job working with peasants in a French vineyard. The suffering she saw and personally experienced left a lasting mark on her.

Through her life Weil's health had not been good. She suffered attacks of pleurisy and severe headaches. It was while she was experiencing one of these headaches that she first felt the impact of Christ. While recuperating in France from burns received in Spain, she was listening to a Gregorian chant. Through this the joy and bitterness of Christ's passion first impressed her. It was also at this time that a friend introduced her to the poetry of George Herbert, which became a way for her to begin to pray.

In 1943, when France was occupied by Nazi Germany, Weil was living in London. She yearned to rejoin her fellow French citizens but never could. In sympathy for her fellow French citizens she refused to eat any more than a prisoner of war was allowed. As a result of this and her weak constitution, she died in August 1943.

GRAVITY

"Men have the same carnal nature as animals. If a hen is hurt, the others rush upon it, attacking it with their beaks. This phenomenon is as automatic as gravitation" (Weil 1973).

"I must not forget that at certain times when my headaches were raging I had an intense longing to make another human being suffer by hitting him in exactly the same part of his forehead. . . . When in this state, I have several times succumbed to the temptation at least to say words which cause pain. Obedience to the force of gravity. The greatest sin" (Weil 1987).

The key fact of our broken human condition is gravity. This is the metaphor Weil uses to describe how we are bound by our own sin and by the suffering in this world. We may make small attempts to escape, but gravity always pulls us back again. Weil compared this to a person jumping toward the sky. We jump and jump but never escape the force of gravity.

The power of gravity is most keenly felt in the midst of great suffering. As we are weighed down by pain, whether physical or spiritual, we feel God is very far away. If we are the one suffering we lash out. We want to cause the same sort of suffering, as Weil candidly says regarding her own raging headaches. We feel powerless in our own suffering and so we exert self-centered power by causing others pain.

The power of gravity is also at work when we see someone else suffering. The temptation is to rush in upon the sufferer like hens in a chicken yard. Weakness scares us. Gravity causes us to despise, exclude or blame the sufferer. This is our human condition. We cannot help ourselves any more than we can escape the earth's gravitational pull.

We human beings don't readily admit that we are so bound. We like to explain away our sinful nature and the problem of suffering by blaming others or addressing only particular sins. The convenient thing about this is that once the blame is shifted or one particular sin is overcome we can imagine ourselves free, unburdened, no longer weighed down. But our bondage goes on. We are bound by gravity. Only God can free us who are so utterly bound.

GRACE

"God created through love and for love. God did not create anything except love itself, and the means to love. He created love in all its forms. He created beings capable of love from all possible distances. Because no other could do it, he himself went to the greatest possible distance, the infinite distance. This infinite distance between God and God, this supreme tearing apart, this agony beyond all others, this marvel of love, is the crucifixion. Nothing can be further from God than that which has been made accursed" (Weil 1973).

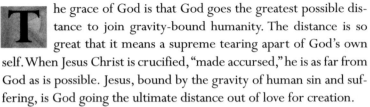

The grace of God is that God goes the greatest possible distance to join gravity-bound humanity. The distance is so great that it means a supreme tearing apart of God's own self. When Jesus Christ is crucified, "made accursed," he is as far from God as is possible. Jesus, bound by the gravity of human sin and suffering, is God going the ultimate distance out of love for creation.

124

Weil sheds new light on the familiar word *grace*. Grace is the supreme "tearing apart" of God. God, powerful creator of all that there is, is loving enough to lay down all that power and submit himself to the force of gravity. In Jesus the crucified God becomes the victim of gravity. Grace means God becomes the accursed and suffering servant, joining us where we are.

In the world of human affairs, being the victim, the weak one, seems so insignificant and ineffective. Weil knows this is not the way the world wants to operate. Similar to Jesus' parable of the yeast, which leavens the whole lump, Weil compares God's grace to a catalyst, which "operates by their mere presence in chemical reactions." God's "supreme tearing apart" means that the world will never be the same again. This act becomes the catalyst that creates our love of God and love of neighbor.

God is the only one who could submit to the force of gravity, take it upon himself in Jesus Christ and continue to love. God's love is stronger than the force of gravity. Because it is, we have the sure hope that gravity cannot keep us in bondage forever. God has bridged the distance, suffered and died, but continued to love. Grace is at work in our world.

WAITING

"Notice that in the Gospels there is never, unless I am mistaken, question of a search for God by man. In all the parables it is the Christ who seeks men. . . . Or again, a man finds the Kingdom of God as if by chance, and then, but only then, he sells all" (Weil 1976).

Weil believed that God in Christ was seeking her and all others. Therefore she waits for God, trusting that God will find her. Such waiting requires great humility. Waiting acknowledges that we are gravity-bound creatures and cannot leap up to God. It also acknowledges that it is God who establishes the relationship and not the actions of our own searching for God.

But, how hard it is for us human beings to wait! Waiting means giving up control of a situation or a relationship. It means trusting in another to act faithfully. We would be more comfortable with searching—at least then we are doing something and have the illusion of being somewhat in control. Weil counsels us, though, to be wary of our searching for God. We tend to settle for what is comfortable, self-serving, and manageable. God is none of these.

Yet waiting is not simply inactivity. Weil herself speaks of wrestling with God out of "pure regard for the truth." She dedicated her life to thinking about and wrestling with faith issues. This was not a means by which to reach God. Instead it shows her trust in God to reach her. As she says with great faith, even if we turn aside from Christ to go toward the truth, "one will not go far before falling into his arms."

The Scriptures also call us to wait for God. But there too waiting is not simply inactivity. It means continuing to live faithfully in the face of evil. We seek to understand and to serve out of faith in God. All this is done as God leads us, done in God's name, according to God's way of doing things.

We are called to be waiting people. Wait, let God establish your path by God's word, especially the Word-in-the-flesh, Jesus Christ. Wait courageously, asking the hard questions and wrestling for the truth. The Lord Jesus is already there for you.

AFFLICTION

"Affliction hardens and discourages us because, like a red hot iron, it stamps the soul to its very depths with the scorn, the disgust, and even the self-hatred and sense of guilt and defilement that crime logically should produce but actually does not. Evil dwells in the heart of the criminal without being felt there. It is felt in the heart of the man who is afflicted and innocent."

"Men struck down by affliction are at the foot of the Cross, almost at the greatest possible distance from God" (Weil 1973).

For Weil, true affliction is distinguished by the depth to which it sears the soul. We feel abandoned by God, misunderstood by our neighbor and even disgusted with ourselves. We blame ourselves and feel guilty about our own suffering. True affliction is never sought by the one who suffers. Such seeking would make it a self-serving project in which we maintain control.

Weil struggled her whole life with her own personal affliction in the form of poor health. She was also very sensitive to the suffering of others. She has no cure for affliction but does put it in the Christian context by relating it to the Christian life.

Weil wrote that the greatness of Christianity "lies in the fact that it does not seek a supernatural remedy for suffering but a supernatural use for it." Jesus did not come to offer us some miraculous escape from physical and spiritual affliction. Rather he came to endure it. In Christ, God joins us in our affliction, experiencing the same great distance from God and neighbor that we do. Still, Christ continues to love both God and neighbor. This is the supernatural use of affliction, to enter it and endure it in love. Such stubborn love breaks the seemingly crushing power of suffering.

In daily life, Christians are not exempt from affliction. It will come. There is no easy explanation for the why, where, or when of it. It is a soul-tearing experience but we have reason to hope and endure. Great suffering does not mean God has abandoned us. When Christians do find themselves in true suffering, their highest calling is to refrain from ceasing to love. Pray for the strength to love in the face of affliction.

PRAYER

"Prayer consists of attention. It is the orientation of all the attention of which the soul is capable toward God. The quality of the attention counts for much in the quality of the prayer. Warmth of heart cannot make up for it" (Weil 1973).

Directing all our attention to God through prayer is a prime way to submit ourselves to God. The prayer does not have to be long, outstanding in warmth or eloquence. Rather, humble submission in prayer means "suspending our thought, leaving it detached, empty, and ready to be penetrated. . . ." We do not focus on what we have to say but come waiting for God.

To focus all our attention on God is humility. And such humility is a victory over evil in ourselves. Weil understood that part of every human being resists focusing on God. Our own concerns, our own schedules, our own goals keep ourselves at the center of our attention. To focus our attention on God, especially through prayer, is to begin to destroy this evil self-centeredness. This is why the attention we pay to God is far more important than the particular prayer we pray or the amount of time we spend praying.

Weil often prayed the Lord's Prayer with great attention. She prayed as she worked in the vineyards of France as well as during times of solitude. She wrote that she had to limit herself to two recitations a day of the Lord's Prayer because its effect was so overpowering. Prayer became especially important to Weil during her times of intense physical suffering. Focusing beyond her own pain to God, praying kept Weil's suffering from overwhelming her and cutting her off from God.

We must be careful, though, not to see prayer as some magical way to coerce God into doing what we want. Weil saw it as a means by which God draws near to us. When this happens God's own purity touches us. To be touched by God keeps us in a right relationship with God. Our own suffering, our own problems and projects no longer overwhelm us.

JUSTICE

"The supernatural virtue of justice consists of behaving exactly as though there were equality when one is the stronger in an unequal relationship. Exactly, in every respect, including the slightest details of accent and attitude, for a detail may be enough to place the weaker party in the condition of matter, which on this occasion naturally belongs to him, just as the slightest shock causes water that has remained liquid below freezing to solidify" (Weil 1973).

Weil realized that our living in equality does not happen naturally; that is why she calls it a "supernatural virtue." Justice and equality become possible by the grace of God. When we act justly by refusing to act or speak in a superior manner we are mirroring God's original generosity in creation. Just as God consented to give life to us, so we are called to give life to others. This happens when we treat each other as equals.

Treating another as an equal means refusing to use our position of strength over one not as strong. Weil saw that special privileges upset the balance of justice by creating distinctions of worth among people and robbing individuals of their God-given dignity. In response to this she developed the notion of counterbalancing.

Counterbalancing means that wherever there is unequal balance God's people must be ready to add weight to the lighter side to achieve balance or equality. Therefore we cannot identify ourselves with any one group or state permanently. Our vocation is to seek a balance, not to promote one group for all time.

Such balancing happens on the cross. God in Christ comes down in order to raise us up, we who are so weighed down by the suffering and evil in the world. Only God could lift the world in the face of all evil. God alone is humble and loving enough to shed all power to come and join us where we are. We are not called to raise the entire world up as God has done, but we are called to act as a balance in order to lift up individuals or groups.

Who is denied justice and equality? Pray for the humility to meet others as equals so that there may be justice in our workplaces, our homes, our world.

UPROOTEDNESS

"Money destroys human roots wherever it is able to penetrate, by turning desire for gain into the sole motive. It easily manages to outweigh all other motives, because the effort it demands of the mind is so very much less. Nothing is so clear and so simple as a row of figures" (Weil 1979).

As the world became increasingly mechanized and industrialized, Weil saw how this was destroying people's ties to the land, their work, and their families. All these things were being made subservient to money or material possessions. Weil saw the world as being "submerged in materialism" (1973).

In today's society we tend to define someone's importance by how much they earn. Many people make huge sacrifices in order to earn larger salaries to buy more things. In our scramble for money and the comfort and prestige it brings, we've sacrificed a certain quality of life.

129

Not only have our roots to our homes been damaged but also our roots to our environment. As we debate the care and protection of our land and air, we drag our feet when we learn it will cost us money to care and preserve it. So often the outcome of the argument is determined by the answer to: "How much will this cost?" As Weil says, "Nothing is *so* clear and *so* simple as a row of figures."

It is true that it is simpler to measure everything in terms of dollars and cents. But the price we pay is a great one. We cut (uproot) ourselves from the blessings God would give us through the land, family, and community.

The human soul needs to be rooted. We belong to this good earth, to family and community and finally, above all, to God. These roots tell us who we are, where we've come from and where we are going. A simple row of figures can never give us so much.

Jesus warns us of the dangers love of money poses to our faith and our relationships with others. His encounter with Zacchaeus, the rich and hated tax-collector, shows us how one person was rerooted in God and his community. Pray, so not to fall for such deceptive and empty simplicity.

BEAUTY AND NATURE

"It is true that there is little mention of the beauty of the world in the Gospel. But in so short a text, which as Saint John says, is very far from containing all that Christ taught, the disciples no doubt thought it unnecessary to put in anything so generally accepted.

"It does, however, come up on two occasions. Once Christ tells us to contemplate and imitate the lilies of the field and the birds of the air, in their indifference as to the future and their docile acceptance of destiny; and another time he invites us to contemplate and imitate the indiscriminate distribution of rain and sunlight" (Weil 1973).

eil sees God secretly present in the beauty of the world. She says of this beauty that it is "Christ's tender smile for us coming through matter" (1973). Christ himself also speaks of the beauty of the lilies and the birds to help us understand the workings of God. We are to follow Christ's lead.

To contemplate the beauty of creation requires self-denial. That is, we need to come to the beauty of creation with humility, refusing to exert power and control. When we do this, that we mirror God's own attitude toward the beauty of this world. God created it, but consents not to arbitrarily command it, even though God has the power to do so. When we come to beauty in humility, then we can be touched by God's presence in it.

In our present day, many have experienced Christ's tender smile through the beauty of the world. Weil recognizes that this beauty is the only way many allow God to touch them today. We are often more willing to see God in the beauty of nature than we are to meet God in worship or our neighbor. This does not mean we stop with nature but it does say that it may be an appropriate place to start for anyone who has trouble seeing God anywhere.

Christ bids us to consider the beauty of the lilies and birds in order to understand the love of God. Where and when can you do this? Time and humility are required but in the splendor of the wild flowers you will find an image of the extravagance of grace; in the vastness of the sky you will find an image of the great love of God.

JOY

"We know then that joy is the sweetness of contact with the love of God. . . . Joy and suffering are two equally precious gifts both of which must be savored to the full, each one in its purity, without trying to mix them. Through joy, the beauty of the world penetrates our soul. Through suffering it penetrates our body. We could no more become friends of God through joy alone than one becomes a ship's captain by studying books on navigation" (Weil 1973).

*J*oy is not a world Weil uses frequently. When she does, it is connected with contact with God. One of the ways she talks about this happening is through the beauty of the world. Another way this happens is in our contact with God's love through worship and especially the Lord's Supper. As with beauty, the earthly points beyond itself to God. As God meets us in the bread and wine, we have joy.

Joy never fully describes the Christian experience. Weil speaks of joy and suffering as "two equally precious gifts." We cannot know one without knowing the other. In other writings she puts it this way: "Suffering is still to joy what hunger is to food" (Weil 1987). Suffering creates our appetite or longing for contact with God, which brings us joy. But neither of these is to be actively sought. This would be especially true of suffering. True suffering is never our own project, it simply comes. If it is our own project then it is a self-serving one, which only leads us to focus on ourselves and not God. The focus must be on God in order to experience true joy.

Weil would counsel us not to settle for counterfeit joy in the form of earthly pleasures or comfort. Our joy is found only in the love of God, which comes to us. We are most hungry for such love in the midst of suffering. It is as we suffer that our gaze rests upon a suffering God who also comes to save us.

Pray for this sturdy joy.

NEIGHBOR

"Christ taught us that the supernatural love of our neighbor is the exchange of compassion and gratitude which happens in a flash between two beings, one possessing and the other deprived of human personality. One of the two is only a little piece of flesh, naked, inert, and bleeding beside a ditch; he is nameless; no one knows anything about him. Those who pass by this thing scarcely notice it, and a few minutes afterward do not even know that they saw it. Only one stops and turns his attention toward it. The actions that follow are just the automatic effect of this moment of attention. The attention is creative. But at the moment when it is engaged it is a renunciation. This is true, at least, if it is pure. The man accepts to be diminished by concentrating on an expenditure of energy, which will not extend his own power but will give existence to a being other than himself . . ." (Weil 1973).

W eil writes of the parable of the Good Samaritan. In it Jesus teaches us what it means to love our neighbor— attention and renunciation. This is how Christ first loved us. Out of love he renounced his power and glory to undergo the sin and evil of this world. Because of Christ this same love now flows through us to our neighbor, anyone who is deprived of full human personality, anyone whose suffering goes unnoticed and is not treated as a full and equal human being. The naked, bleeding man in the ditch is all of these.

To love our neighbor is to pay attention to anyone who is in a weaker position than we are. That sounds so simple! But attention is more than just looking at something or someone. Attention is creative. It restores the full humanity, full equality of the sufferer. This takes time, concentration, and energy away from us. To pay attention is to deny ourselves, diminish ourselves in order to restore another human being.

In this way attention goes beyond charity. Charity is easy. We give leftovers and fleeting moments of notice and time. When we do this we are like those who walk by the bleeding man in the ditch. We received more than charity from God, and we are called to give more than that to our neighbor.

THOMAS MERTON

Mary Schramm

THE ONE PERSON WHOSE LIFE AND WRITINGS HAVE PROBABLY changed attitudes toward spirituality, monasticism, and contemplation more than any other is Father Louis of Gethsemani Abbey, Kentucky. He is better known to the world as Thomas Merton (1915–1968). In his autobiography, *Seven Storey Mountain,* and other early writings, he wrote with a tone of triumphalism. Merton's major contributions, however, came from the mature Catholic monk who bridges East and West, and who is open to the truth of Protestantism and to secular writers.

As a young man, he attended Columbia University in New York City. Merton describes himself as a "worldly man" in these years, drinking beer and writing for the campus humor magazine.

Merton's reading included the works of St. Thomas, and he became more and more interested in religion. In 1938, at twenty-three years of age, he was baptized into the Catholic faith. As he began the search for his vocation, he taught English, worked on a newspaper, and volunteered at the *Catholic Worker.* A visit to Gethsemani Abbey planted a seed, and when he was twenty-six he entered the Trappist abbey as a novice.

As the years went by, Merton felt more and more called to a solitary life and began to live in a small hermitage away from the abbey. He became a prolific writer. More than sixty of his books have been published. Hundreds of articles, a lifetime of extensive correspondence, and unpublished journals are also part of the Merton heritage.

This monk was a poet and a social critic. He had an artist's eye as evidenced by his sketches and excellent photography. In his writings one finds a combination of humor, deep faith, joy at simple things, and a righteous anger at the injustice in the world.

He could laugh at theologians who were not happy unless "God was a problem," and convinced many of his readers that to be contemplative is not to see a different world, but to see *this* world differently.

The selections from his writings that follow sample the breadth of Merton's interests and concerns. Had Merton been alive today, I feel certain he would have been more inclusive in his language because his insights, like his faith, reflected contemporary issues.

SANITY

"I am beginning to realize that 'sanity' is no longer a value or an end in itself. If modern man were a little less sane, a little more doubtful, perhaps there might be the possibility of survival. But if he is sane, too sane, perhaps we must say that in a society like ours the worst insanity is to be totally without anxiety, totally 'sane'" (Merton 1966).

nce on the news was a report of an Arkansas man who shot and killed sixteen people. One watched with horror as bodies were removed from shallow graves and trunks of abandoned cars. The man had to be insane, we said to each other.

The dictionary defines *sanity* as being able to make rational judgments, showing good sense. Adolf Eichmann, it was pronounced at his trial, was perfectly sane. Merton writes that he was obedient, loyal, and had a profound respect for the law. In his sanity, Eichmann was able to thoughtfully send six million Jews to their deaths.

In 1945 the United States deliberately used a Roman Catholic cathedral as ground zero and dropped a bomb that killed thousands of Japanese people. We make certain the men and women who control our missile systems are perfectly sane folks who pass psychological tests and make good sense out of the Rorschach inkblot designs.

Who is sane?

Cultural assumptions of sanity often seem to be on a collision course with the sanity of God. The wisdom of God contradicts the sanity of an arms race. Is it sane to return love for hatred, nonviolence for violent acts against us?

The monk from his hillside at Gethsemani Abbey in Kentucky was an astute observer of humanity. Paul spoke to this when he wrote to the Corinthians: "Where is the wise [person]? . . . Has not God made foolish the wisdom of the world? . . . For Jews demand signs and Greeks seek wisdom, but we preach Christ crucified, a stumbling block to Jews and folly to Gentiles, but to those who are called, both Jews and Greeks, Christ the power of God and the wisdom of God. For the foolishness of God is wiser than men, and the weakness of God is stronger than men" (1 Cor. 1:20–25).

DESPAIR

here are many reasons, I suppose, why we neglect solitude. We claim outside distractions, a family needing our
attention, a job that makes many demands. Or is our neglect of solitude a symptom of a deeper malaise—the fear of facing
ourselves and looking hard at the despair in our lives? Sometimes
our solitude demands that we move into the darkness of our life
instead of denying or avoiding it.

Both Jesus and John the Baptizer had their desert experiences.
They embraced despair and temptation in these times of solitude
and the call upon their lives was renewed. All of us experience
times of emptiness and that flat feeling when we wonder if God is
indeed in charge of our world or cares for us at all.

Merton was acutely aware of this human crisis. He wrote: *"The
desert is the home of despair. And despair now is everywhere. Let us not think*

*that our interior solitude consists in the acceptance of defeat. We cannot escape
anything by consenting tacitly to be defeated. Despair is an abyss without bottom. Do not think to close it by consenting to it and trying to forget you have
consented. This, then, is our desert: to live facing despair, but not to consent. To
trample it down under hope in the cross. To wage war against despair unceasingly. That war is our wilderness. If we wage it courageously, we will find Christ
at our side. If we cannot face it we will never find Him"* (Merton 1956).

The opposite of faith is not unbelief. The opposite of faith is
despair. To despair is to disbelieve the resurrection or to forget that in
his suffering and his resurrection Christ defeated the powers of evil.
God will rule. Jesus knows what it is like for us to despair. In the garden and on the cross he cried out to a God who seemed to have forgotten him. That is why Christ is always with us in our struggle.

"Who shall separate us from the love of Christ? Shall tribulation,
or distress, or persecution, or famine, or peril? . . . No, in all these
things we are more than conquerors through him who loved us. For
I am sure that neither death, nor life, nor angels, nor principalities,
nor things present, nor things to come, nor powers, nor height, nor
depth, nor anything else in all creation, will be able to separate us
from the love of God in Christ Jesus our Lord" (Rom. 8:35–39).

RAIN

One evening Merton left the monastery and sloshed his way through the cornfields to his special hermitage in the woods. He cooked some oatmeal and toasted a piece of bread over the log fire. It was raining and on the metal roof he reflected on its sound and meaning: *"Let me say this before rain becomes a utility that they can plan and distribute for money. By 'they' I mean the people who cannot understand that rain is a festival, who think that what has no price has no value, that what cannot be sold is not real, so that the only way to make something* actual *is to place it on the market. The time will come when they will sell you even your rain. I celebrate its gratuity"* (Merton 1966).

Rain as a festival, a pure celebration! It has value simply because it is. It is gift. It has no price tag and its worth cannot be calculated. It is accepted purely as a grace from a gracious God.

How rare to see something as valuable that cannot be bought or sold. There are few enough things in our world that we celebrate simply because they are. Even our worth as individuals usually depends upon what we possess or how well we are liked.

Writer James Carroll says that to be called useless in society is the thing that stirs within us our deepest fear, and so we attack the uselessness in others. But it is in our uselessness that we are human. Our humanity is a celebration simply because God created us.

Merton, the poet, ends his essay, "Rain and the Rhinoceros," with these words: *"The rain has stopped. The afternoon sun slants through the pine trees; and how useless needles smell in the clean air!*

"A dandelion, long out of season, has pushed itself into bloom between the smashed leaves of last summer's day lilies. The valley resounds with the totally uninformative talk of creeks and the wild water.

"Then the quails begin their sweet whistling in the wet bushes. Their noise is absolutely useless, and so is the delight I take in it. There is nothing I would rather hear, not because it is a better noise than other noises, but because it is the voice of the present moment, the present festival" (Merton 1966).

The earth is the Lord's and the fullness thereof. Let us rejoice and be glad in it. Amen

CONTENTMENT

have learned, in whatever state I am, to be content. I know how to be abased, and I know how to abound; in any and all circumstances I have learned the secret of facing plenty and hunger, abundance and want. I can do all things in him who strengthens me" (Phil. 4:11–13).

Contentment is that quality that allows us to live fully in the present, seeing the possibilities and the joys at hand. How much of our energy and time is channeled into planning for future events, future security, future prospects. Our car is never quite right, our apartment is not quite large enough, our salary is never adequate, and our work is never as fulfilling as we want. Our children aren't as gifted as we had hoped, our spouse not as romantic as we dreamed, and our health not perfect.

In *Conjectures of a Guilty Bystander*, Merton writes: *"Why can we not be content with the secret happiness that God offers us without consulting the rest of the world? If we are fools enough to remain at the mercy of the people who want to sell us happiness, it will be impossible for us ever to be content with anything. How would they profit if we became content? . . . The last thing a salesman wants is for the buyer to become content. You are no use in our affluent society unless you are always just about to grasp what you never have.*

"The Greeks were not as smart as we are. In their primitive way they put Tantalus in hell. Madison Avenue, on the contrary, would convince us that Tantalus is in heaven" (Merton 1968).

Our own hell surrounds us when the tantalizing glitter of a materialistic world robs us of the contentment God has to offer. God's world is a beautiful world. If we have eyes to see and ears to hear we are doubly blessed. And if we have food to sustain our bodies, a place to rest, someone to love and meaningful work to do we are richer than the richest person on earth.

God's secret of contentment is for us to become aware of how much we are loved and that God gives us people who need us.

Gracious God, let me learn the meaning of the word "enough." Amen

RECONCILIATION

"I have learned that an age in which politicians talk about peace is an age in which everybody expects war; the great men of the earth would not talk of peace so much if they did not secretly believe it possible, with one more war, *to annihilate their enemies forever. Always, 'after just one more war' it will dawn, the new era of love; but first everybody who is hated must be eliminated. For hate, you see, is the mother of their kind of love"* (Merton 1961a).

 Planning and executing just one more war is not new to 20th-century people. The sin of thinking that peace will come if we can only destroy the enemy or threaten their existence has been with humanity since creation.

After the Civil War, Abraham Lincoln was talking about being reconciled to the South and one member of his cabinet, Thaddeus Stevens, banged his fist on the table and said, "Mr. President, I think enemies are to be destroyed!" Mr. Lincoln quietly responded, "Do I not destroy my enemy when I make him my friend?"

God chose to reconcile us while we were enemies of God by the self-giving love of Christ on a cross. The way God relates to enemies is our model for reconciliation. Forgiveness, understanding, and compassion are the marks of what it means to follow Jesus.

"To the extent that you are free to choose evil, you are not free. An evil choice destroys freedom," Merton wrote. Our freedom is to align ourselves with the will of God. God's will for us is to be reconciled to our neighbor, our enemy, and our family member.

It is difficult to describe the peacefulness that is ours when we take the first step in being reconciled to one from whom we are estranged. This peace that passes understanding is God's gift, who always calls us to love instead of hate. God never commands us to live a certain way without furnishing the spiritual resources to do so.

"But now in Christ Jesus you who once were far off have been brought near in the blood of Christ. For he is our peace, who has made us both one, and has broken down the dividing wall of hostility" (Eph. 2:13–14).

Give me the spiritual resources, Holy Spirit, to be reconciled to my enemies. Amen

HUMILITY

"In great saints you will find that perfect humility and perfect integrity coincide. . . . The saint is unlike everybody else precisely because he is humble. . . . Humility consists in being precisely the person you are before God, and since no two people are alike, if you have the humility to be yourself you will not be like anyone else in the whole universe." (Merton 1961b).

 omehow in our religious training, we have been led to believe humility and groveling are synonymous. Our "worm" theology that mistakenly passes for humbleness often prevent us from experiencing the grace of an integrated life.

Each of us was created with a unique combination of gifts and abilities. When we deny these gifts we deny our very essence. We give God glory when we accept ourselves as the person God intended for us to be—a unique created individual.

When we accept ourselves with our special gifts (and limitations), we are able to forget self and reach out to others. We do not flaunt who we are, but accept God's gifts to us and begin to use those gifts for others. We can stop searching for ways to respond to God's love and begin to be who we are.

"Hurry," Merton said, "ruins saints as well as artists." How like us to be discontented with small steps, small results, and to want immediate gratification and success. We live our lives so hurriedly that we rarely take the time to discover who we are. It is when we shut up for awhile that God's Spirit within us can be heard.

"I bid every one among you not to think of himself more highly than he ought to think, but to think with sober judgment, each according to the measure of faith which God has assigned him. For as in one body we have many members, and all the members do not have the same function, so we, though many, are one body in Christ, and individually members one of another. Having gifts that differ according to the grace given to us, let us use them" (Rom. 12:3–6).

Thank you, parent God, for the gift of who I am. Keep me from selfish use of my gifts. Amen

PRAYER

A friend called today. "This has been a hard week," he said. "I need your support and your prayers."

What is prayer? How am I supposed to pray? Does it make any difference? What if I can't seem to pray?

The most helpful advice I have read comes from spiritual director John Chapman: "Pray as you can. Don't pray as you can't." Then he adds, "The less you pray the worse it goes."

When Merton was asked to speak at a conference on "how to pray," he was very blunt. "If you want to pray, begin to pray. Start praying. Pray." In our busy lives we are often tempted to say that all of life is a prayer. Everything we do is for the glory of God. No one led a fuller life than Jesus and yet we read in Mark 1:35 that "in the morning, a great while before day, he rose and went out to a lonely place, and there he prayed." In between healing and preaching, Jesus knew the importance of a time for intimacy with God.

For Merton, prayer is the time "we abandon our inertia, our egoism and submit entirely to the demands of the Spirit, praying earnestly for help, and giving ourselves generously to every effort asked of us by God" (Merton 1971). Later Merton writes, "The theology of prayer begins when we understand that we are in trouble." Prayer begins with those moments of honesty when we stand before God, confessing our inability to make sense out of life, and abandoning our wills to the one who created and redeemed us.

"Prayer does not blind us to the world, but it transforms our vision of the world and makes us see it, all people, and all the history of mankind in the light of God." Prayer is not an escape but a way of "keeping oneself in the presence of God and of reality, rooted in one's own inner truth."

For those of us who feel immature in our prayer life, Merton has a comforting word. "We do not want to be beginners. But let us be convinced of the fact that we will never be anything else but beginners all our life!" There are no short cuts to a life of prayer. One begins to pray, and by the grace of God we come in touch with the source of our life.

CONTEMPLATION

ne of several books by Thomas Merton destined to become a classic of spiritual readings is *New Seeds of Contemplation*. Contemplation is a word often misunderstood even in religious circles. One would hardly consider encouraging your child to grow up to be a contemplative. We think of a contemplative as an oddity, one withdrawn from the world or in some state of constant religious ecstasy.

Merton was aware of these prejudices and not only tried to define contemplation, but devoted a chapter to what contemplation *is not*. I found his distinctions helpful.

Contemplation is *the highest expression of man's intellectual and spiritual life. It is that life itself, fully awake, fully active, fully aware that it is alive. It is spiritual wonder. It is spontaneous awe at the sacredness of life, of being.*

Contemplation is not *something that can be taught, explained, hinted at, suggested, pointed to, symbolized. It can only be experienced.*

Contemplation is *above all, awareness of the reality of the source of life and of our very being. It knows the Source obscurely, inexplicably, but with a certitude that goes both beyond reason and beyond simple faith. For contemplation is a kind of spiritual vision to which both reason and faith aspire.*

Contemplation is *more than a consideration of abstract truths about God, more even than affective meditation on the things we believe. It is awakening enlightenment and the amazing intuitive grasp by which love gains certitude of God's creative and dynamic intervention in daily life* (Merton 1961b).

Merton is trying to help us become acutely aware of all of life. Perhaps a comment made by an Anglican Benedictine to my husband best sums it up. The monk and my husband were walking around the grounds of the monastery in Michigan and he said, "People come here and expect they will find that contemplation comes after years of disciplined training. They think it is some highly developed technique. I tell them they can be a contemplative beginning today. They must begin to look at everything through the lens of their faith in Christ."

God of love, open my eyes and my ears to the beauty and the anguish of the world you care for. Amen

HAPPINESS

"It is not that someone else is preventing you from living happily; you your-self do not know what you want. Rather than admit this, you pretend that someone is keeping you from exercising your liberty. Who is this? It is you yourself" (Merton 1961b).

 t is so convenient to blame others for our inability to be happy. Many of us still blame our parents for imperfect childhoods, find spouses an easy target for our discontent, or imagine our present job and coworkers the reason for our miserable life. This will always be the case when we allow any one person or situation to fully control our level of contentment, or when we forget who and whose we are.

In *No Man Is an Island* Merton writes, "We cannot be happy if we expect to live all the time at the highest peak of intensity. Happiness is not a matter of intensity, but of balance and order and rhythm and harmony."

143

I suspect that it is easier to find this balance in a monastery than in our modern world of frantic haste with appointments to keep and deadlines to meet. For Merton, the balance included work and worship, study and leisure.

As we look closely at Merton's values, we become aware that it truly is in those times of want and pain that we draw closer to God. As for the monotony, Merton described the monastery as being "deliberately boring" because when we are no longer distracted, we are able to turn more fully to God in prayer.

Not long ago I realized I had a "boring evening at home." No one was there, nothing good on television, no book that interested me. I was blaming others for my unhappiness.

For three hours, I did nothing but pray, cry, listen, and look deeply into my heart. With gratitude I recommitted my life to the God who created and redeemed me. The peace that passes understanding comes alive in moments like these.

For a time of prayer, sit quietly, eyes closed, conscious of your breathing. Spend fifteen minutes aware of God's Spirit within you.

GOD'S LOVE

"It is God's love that warms me in the sun and God's love that sends the cold rain. It is God's love that feeds me in the bread I eat and God that feeds me also by hunger and fasting.

"It is the love of God that sends the winter days when I am cold and sick, and the hot summer when I labor and my clothes are full of sweat; but it is God who breathes on me with light winds off the river and in breezes out of the wood.

"It is God's love that speaks to me in the birds and streams, and all these things are seeds sent to me from his will. If these seeds would take root in my liberty, and if his will would grow from my freedom, I would become the love that he is, and my harvest would be his glory and my own joy" (Merton 1961b).

It is the contemplative who can acknowledge the presence of God's care and love in all facets of life—from the sweat that soaks our clothes in the hot summertime to the cold rain of autumn. All creation gives God glory and does so without thought, without labor, and without awareness. Nature praises God simply because it *is*.

But what about us, Merton asks? We are called to be holy. "Our vocation is not simply to be, but to work together with God in the creation of our own life, our own identity, our own destiny."

Paul speaks of this paradox when he writes, "Work out your own salvation with fear and trembling; for God is at work in you, both to will and to work for his good pleasure" (Phil. 2:12).

By God's spirit we come to know God's will and are free to respond to that will. We can become cocreators with God, helping to create our identity and become the person we were created to be, or we can submit to the illusion that we will find joy outside of God's will for our lives. "We are not very good at recognizing illusions," Merton writes, "least of all the ones we cherish about ourselves. . . . A life devoted to the cult of this shadow is what is called a life of sin."

Come, Holy Spirit, and let God's love flow through me. Awaken me to that love in all of life. Amen

144

BIBLIOGRAPHY

Anselm

Prayers and Meditations. Translated by Benedicta Ward. New York: Penguin Books, 1973.

Augustine

Corpus Christianorum. Series Latina. Turnholt, Belgium: Brepols, 1886.

Nicene and Post Nicene Fathers. Augustine Series, Vols. 1–3. Buffalo, New York: Christian Literature Company, 1954.

Patrologiae Cursus Completus. Edited by J. P. Migne. Series Latina, Vols. 34–37. Evanston, Ill.: Adlers Foreign Books, 1965–71.

Bodo, Murray

The Journey and the Dream. Cincinnati: St. Anthony Messenger Press, 1972.

The Way of St. Francis. New York: Image Books, 1984.

Bonhoeffer, Dietrich

The Cost of Discipleship. Translated by R. H. Fuller; revised by Irmgard Booth. New York: Macmillan, 1966.

Ethics. Translated by Neville Horton Smith; edited by Eberhard Bethge. New York: Macmillan, 1965a.

Letters and Papers from Prison, ed. 4. Translated by R. H. Fuller; revised by Irmgard Booth. New York: Macmillan, 1965b.

Life Together. Translated by John W. Doberstein. New York and Evanston: Harper & Row, 1954.

Meditating on the Word. Edited and translated by David McI. Gracie. Cambridge, Mass.: Cowley Publications, 1986.

Psalms: The Prayer Book of the Bible. Translated by James Burtness. Minneapolis: Augsburg, 1970.

Brother Lawrence

The Practice of the Presence of God. Translated by G. Symons. Cincinnati: Forward Movement Publications, 1941.

The Practice of the Presence of God. Translated by John J. Delaney. Garden City, N.Y.: Image Books, 1977.

Bunyan, John

The Spiritual Riches of John Bunyan. Edited by Thomas Kepler. Cleveland: World Publishing, 1952.

Cornelia, Jessey

The Prayer of Cosa. Minneapolis: Winston Press, 1985.

Doyle, Brendan

Meditations with Julian of Norwich. Santa Fe: Bear and Company, 1983.

Hallesby, O.

Prayer. Translated by C. J. Carlsen. Minneapolis: Augsburg, 1931.

Julian of Norwich

Revelations of Divine Love. New York: Viking Penguin, 1966.

Kierkegaard, Søren

Søren Kierkegaard's Journal and Papers. Vols. I–VII. Bloomington, Ind.: Indiana University Press, 1967–78.

Works of Love. New York: Harper, 1962.

Luther, Martin

Commentary on St. Paul's Epistle to the Galatians. Revised and edited by Philip S. Watson. London: James Clarke and Co., Ltd.; reprinted in *Martin Luther: Selections from His Writings.* Edited by John Dillenberger. Garden City, N.Y.: Anchor Books, 1961.

Luther Discovers the Gospel. Translated by Uuras Saarnivaara. St. Louis: Concordia; reprinted in *The Reformation: A Narrative History Related by Contemporary Observers and Participants.* Edited by Hans J. Hillerbrand. Grand Rapids, Mich.: Baker Book House, 1973.

LuthersWerke, vol. 45, 1911.

LuthersWerke, vol. 49, 1913.

LuthersWerke, vol. 51, 1914.

Luther's Works, Vol. 31. Edited and revised by Harold J. Grimm. Translated by W. A. Lambert. Philadelphia: Fortress Press; reprinted in Dillenberger's *Martin Luther: Selections from His Writings,* 1957.

Luther'sWorks, vol. 51. Edited andTranslated by JohnW. Doberstein. Philadelphia: Fortress Press, 1959.

Luther'sWorks, vol. 52. Edited by Hans J. Hillerbrand. Philadelphia: Fortress Press, 1974.

Martin Luthers Werke, Kritische Gesamtausgabe, vol. 32. Weimar: Hermann Böhlaus Nachfolger. Author's translation, 1906D.

Merton, Thomas

Conjectures of a Guilty Bystander. NewYork: Image Books, 1968.

Contemplative Prayer. NewYork: Image Books, 1971.

Emblems of a Season of Fury. NewYork: New Directions, 1961a.

New Seeds of Contemplation. NewYork: New Directions, 1961b.

Raids on the Unspeakable. NewYork: New Directions, 1966.

Thoughts in Solitude. NewYork: New Directions, 1956.

Thomas à Kempis

The Imitation of Christ. NewYork: Hippocrene Books, 1986.

Weil, Simone

Intimations of Christianity Among the Ancient Greeks. London: Routledge & Kegan Paul, Ltd., 1976.

Gravity and Grace. NewYork: Ark Paperbacks, 1987.

The Need for Roots. NewYork: Hippocrene Books, 1979.

Waiting for God. NewYork: Harper Colophone Books, 1973.

ACKNOWLEDGMENTS

Excerpts from *Psalms: A Prayerbook of the Bible* by Dietrich Bonhoeffer, trans. by James Burtness. Used by permission.

Excerpts from *Prayer* by O. Hallesby, trans. by C. J. Carlsen, copyright © 1931. Used by permission.

Excerpt from *Meditating on theWord* by Dietrich Bonhoeffer, edited and trans. by David Mcl. Gracie, copyright © 1986 Cowley Publications (1-800-225-1534; www.cowley.org). Reprinted by permission.

Excerpt from *The Practice of the Presence of God* by Brother Lawrence of the Resurrection, trans. by John J. Delaney, copyright © 1977 by John J. Delaney. Used by permission of Doubleday, a division of Random House, Inc.

Excerpt from *Thoughts in Solitude* by Thomas Merton, copyright © 1956 New Directions Publishing; copyright © 1958 by the Abbey of Our Lady of Gethsemani; copyright renewed 1986 by the Trustees of the Thomas Merton Legacy Trust. Reprinted by permission of Farrar, Straus and Giroux, LLC.

Excerpt from *The Practice of the Presence of God* by Brother Lawrence, translated by G. Symons, copyright © 1941 Forward Movement Publications, Cincinnati, OH, 1-800-543-1813. Reprinted by permission.

Excerpt from *All Creatures of Our God and King* by William Draper, copyright © 1923 J. Curwen & Sons, Ltd. All rights for the U.S. & Canada controlled by G. Schirmer, Inc. (Text by St. Francis of Assisi; English translation and Music Arrangement by William Draper) International copyright secured. All rights reserved. Reprinted by Permission of G. Schirmer, Inc., as agents for J. Curwen & Sons, Ltd.

Excerpt from *The Prayer of Cosa* by Cornelia Jessey, copyright © 1985 by Cornelia Jessey.

Excerpt from *Works of Love* by Soren Kierkegaard and trans. by Howard Hong, English language translation copyright © 1962 by Howard Hong. Reprinted by permission of HarperCollins Publishers, Inc.

Excerpt from *Life Together* by Dietrich Bonhoeffer, trans. by John Doberstein, English translation copyright © 1954 by Harper & Brothers, copyright renewed 1982 by Helen S. Doberstein. Reprinted by permission of HarperCollins Publishers, Inc.

Excerpt from *The Imitation of Christ* by Thomas à Kempis, copyright © 1986. Published by Octagon Books, a division of Hippocrene Books, Inc. Reprinted by permission.

Excerpt from "Eternal Spirit of the Living Christ," copyright © 1974 The Hymn Society. Admin. by Hope Publishing Co., Carol Stream, IL 60188. All rights reserved. Used by permission.

Excerpts from Soren Kierkegaard's Journals and Papers, Volumes 1-VIII, trans. Howard & Edna Hong, copyright © 1967-1978 Indiana University Press. Used by the permission of the publisher.

Other Resources from Augsburg

Steadfast in Your Word edited by Barbara Owen
160 pages, 0-8066-4422-2

This devotional volume of daily reflections from Martin
Luther samples many sources written at various times during
Luther's busy life. The themes include vocation, God's Word,
prayer, faith, good works, music, and the church.

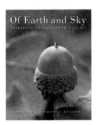

Of Earth and Sky compiled by Thomas Becknell
160 pages, 0-8066-4260-2

Thomas Becknell brings together classic and contemporary
selections from more than eighty of the world's finest writers
to illustrate the seven virtues as they are taught through
nature.

Words of Prayer
128 pages, 0-8066-4246-7

This devotional and meditation tool combines the beauty of
the prayers of Scripture with full-color paintings. The
prayers of Jesus, Mary, Moses, and others illustrate themes
of prayer and praise.

Songs of Praise
128 pages, 0-8066-4171-1

This devotional and meditation tool combines the beauty of
the songs of Scripture with full-color paintings. Each song is
matched with a beautiful work of art by artists such as
Monet and Van Gogh.

Available wherever books are sold.
To order these books directly, contact:
1-800-328-4648 • www.augsburgfortress.org
Augsburg Fortress, Publishers
P.O. Box 1209, Minneapolis, MN 55440-1209